WILD ABOUT DORSET

WILD ABOUT DORSET

THE NATURE DIARY OF A
WEST COUNTRY PARISH

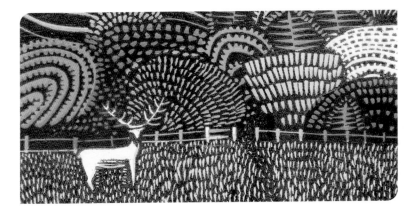

BRIAN JACKMAN

First published in the UK in October 2022 by Bradt Guides Ltd
31a High Street, Chesham, HP5 1BW, England
www.bradtguides.com

Print edition published in the USA by The Globe Pequot Press Inc,
PO Box 480, Guilford, Connecticut 06437-0480

Text copyright © 2022 Brian Jackman
Map copyright © 2022 Bradt Guides

Edited by Ross Dickinson; project managed by Anna Moores

Cover illustration by Liz Somerville (lizsomerville.co.uk)
Design, layout and typesetting by Pepi Bluck
Map by David McCutcheon FBCart.S and Pepi Bluck
Production managed by Sue Cooper, Bradt Guides & Page Bros Ltd
Chapter openers and back cover illustrations © Carry Akroyd
In-text illustrations © shutterstock.com; see page 153 for
individual artists

ISBN: 9781804690321

British Library Cataloguing in Publication Data
A catalogue record for this book is available from the British Library

Digital conversion by www.dataworks.co.in
Printed in the UK by Page Bros Ltd

To Kenneth Allsop

in memoriam.

AUTHOR

Brian Jackman is an award-winning author and travel writer with a lifelong interest in the natural world. He is best known as Britain's foremost writer on African wildlife safaris, but is equally passionate about Dorset, where he has lived since the 1960s. His previous books include *Wild About Britain*, *The Marsh Lions* (with Jonathan Scott), *Savannah Diaries* and *West with the Light: My Life in Nature*, all published by Bradt Guides.

ILLUSTRATORS

Carry Akroyd (carryakroyd.co.uk) is a painter and printmaker, whose landscapes often represent wildlife in the margins of arable farmland. She is a member of the Society of Wildlife Artists, regularly illustrates the 'Bird of the Month' column in *The Oldie* magazine, and is current president of the John Clare Society.

Liz Somerville (lizsomerville.co.uk) is a printmaker whose technique combines a lino- or wood-cut with painted blocks of colour. Her imagery concentrates on landscapes and can be viewed in galleries and at exhibitions across the UK.

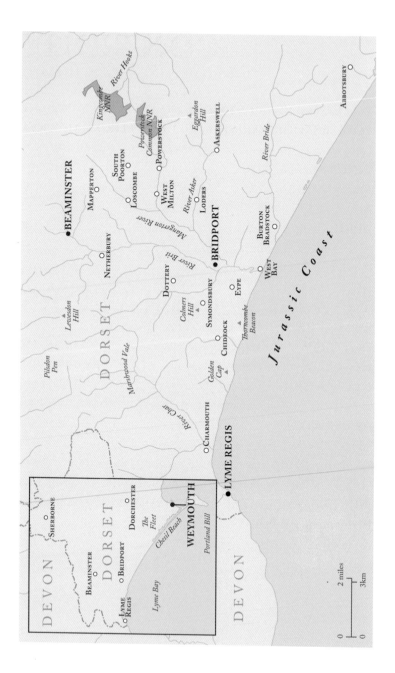

CONTENTS

WELCOME TO WILD WEST DORSET

IT was in September 2014 that I was first invited to write *Wild About Dorset* as a regular column for the *Eggardon and Colmers View*, the excellent little parish magazine which covers not only West Milton where I live, but also the neighbouring villages between Eggardon Hill and the Marshwood Vale. Drawn together for the first time, these monthly snapshots provide a comprehensive portrait of the rich and varied wildlife to be found in West Dorset's miraculously unspoilt countryside and along its dramatic Jurassic Coast.

I first came to Dorset half a lifetime ago on a visit to West Bay – the Broadchurch of ITV's eponymous thriller – and was so struck by its magic that I ended up buying a tumbledown cottage three miles away in the hinterland. At first, I was just a weekender. Now I am a resident and – 40 years on – almost a local.

What I had stumbled upon was not Thomas Hardy's Wessex, still less the genteel world of Jane Austen. Its literary heroes belong to more recent times – to the spirit of John Fowles on the Cobb at Lyme Regis, and above all to Kenneth Allsop, the writer and broadcaster who lived in the Georgian mill in West Milton.

'There is nowhere like it,' declared Allsop, whose book, *In the Country*, describes to perfection its 'tumbled anarchy of hills' and the feeling of being 'swallowed in the remoteness and antiquity of the land.' His words, written more than 30 years ago, still hold true today.

When Hardy wrote *Far from the Madding Crowd* in 1874, Dorset was the poorest county in Britain, locked in an ancient silence in which life for most of its inhabitants moved no faster than the pace of a horse.

In summer, on farms untouched by herbicides, scarlet poppies bloomed in profusion amid the standing corn, as they would on the battlefields where the Great War would soon be fought, and barbed wire was still a novelty. Instead, fields loud with bees and grasshoppers remained enclosed by hand-laid hedgerows.

In the damp valley bottoms, cattle stood up to their udders in buttercups, and high above them, on the steep chalk scarps and the downs beyond, shepherds wandered with their flocks to the long-vanished sound of sheep bells.

It may sound idyllic, but the reality of rural life was different. The labourers who cut the hay and trimmed the hedges lived on a frugal diet of bread and potatoes and Blue Vinny cheese, washed down with tea or cider. Yet even then, Dorset's sense of isolation was ending, and by the time the Great War was over, the county would never be the same again.

Long gone are the toilers in the turnip fields, the steam threshing machines at harvest time and the heavy horses that hauled the wagons. Gone, too, are the lonely downland sheep walks, the flocks that grew fat on their sweet grasses, replaced by fields of rapeseed and the giant pylons of the national grid.

Even in my time, the rich burr of the old men who sat nursing their pints in the flagstone bars of the village pubs has been replaced by the upcountry accents of second-homers. And yet, a century on, so much of Hardy's Wessex survives, an intensely rural corner of England without so much as a mile of motorway. Apart from Poole and Bournemouth's urban sprawl the entire county remains intensely rural, having become one of the last strongholds for wildlife in the southern half of Britain.

At the heart of it lies our own quiet parish, surrounded by a unique landscape of plum-pudding hills and secret combes that sets it apart, almost a separate county with Bridport as its bucolic capital. Apart from the East Devon border it has no hard-and-fast boundaries – only the crumbling sea cliffs of the Jurassic Coast, marching west to Lyme Regis. Inland it melts away somewhere just north of Beaminster.

That is the big picture, but the epicentre – the crème de la crème in landscape terms – lies within a five-mile radius of Powerstock. And although my diary sometimes strays beyond its borders, this is where the main narrative is set.

The best way to approach it is along the Roman road that runs over the downs from Dorchester to Eggardon Hill, the massive Iron Age fortress whose grassy ramparts guard a geological frontier, the great divide between the chalk and the greensand, where the South Country ends and the true West Country begins. Follow it and you will find yourself in one of the last unspoilt corners of rural England.

Brian Jackman
West Milton, Dorset
August 2022

POWERSTOCK PARISH THROUGH THE YEAR

JANUARY

UP at seven and out into a cold midwinter dawn. Last night was bitter, the clear sky pricked by torrents of icy green stars. Now the fields are white. Frozen grass crunching underfoot. Molehills hard as iron, puddles shattering like broken glass and every twig and dead bracken frond bristling with a coat of rime.

Sound carries far in the frosty air: pheasants calling; cows blaring; a tractor coughing into life as the village wakes. Bullfinches pipe in the apple trees and a quick flash of bright cerise gives away a cock bird as he shears off a bud with his stubby bill.

At a quarter past eight the sun nudges over Eggardon's Iron Age ramparts. A sparrowhawk drifts past, skimming at knee height across the ground to disappear over a hedge, and a roebuck feeding in a field is embalmed for a moment in the sudden flood of amber light. Then its horned head goes up and it runs for cover, bounding back into the wood from which it came.

From my hillside vantage point, I look down upon a spectacle of extraordinary beauty. When I left home the village was clear. Now only the church tower is visible, its weathercock glinting in the sun. It has turned into one of those rare mornings when mist lies thick as sheep's wool in the valleys, as if a ghostly tide has come stealing in to drown the tangled combes and hollows, a sea of vapour in which disembodied hills and treetops float like anchored galleons.

It does not last. The mist rises with the sun, thinning as it spreads until Eggardon's gaunt outline no longer stands out sharply but becomes blurred and indistinct and then vanishes altogether. The air moves again after the deep-frozen stillness of the night. Brittle stems that stood motionless now stir as a light breeze begins to creep over the fields. In less than an hour the dawn's fresh-minted brightness has faded. What was miraculous has now become commonplace and I turn for home, suddenly filled with the need for breakfast and the smell of coffee.

❧

IN January, the Dorset winterbournes are in full flow. Bone dry in summer, these seasonal tributaries are among the county's unsung glories, as are all chalk streams with their gin-clear pools and rippling manes of water crowfoot.

There are only 200 such streams in the world and Britain boasts the lion's share. No less than 85 per cent of them are found in England, including the perfect little River Allen that flows through the heart of Wimborne Minster, and the 30 miles of the Frome.

These are names well-known to trout fishermen, unlike our own West Dorset streams whose muddy banks and stony beds sing a different song as they tumble down from the surrounding hills. Yet even here, during the midwinter spates when the rivers rise and the water comes boiling over the weirs, our native brown trout swim upstream to spawn in the gravel redds where they themselves were born.

Brown trout are members of the salmon family. *Salmo trutta* is their Latin name, and those that adopt a different lifestyle, swimming out into the English Channel before they return to spawn, are known as sea trout. With a 20-year lifespan they can weigh up to 20 pounds (9 kilograms), attain a length of 31 inches (78 centimetres), and may try to return every year to spawn.

The West Bay fishermen used to catch them in their trammel nets from time to time. 'They gurt shiners,' they called them, and hid them under the floorboards when they brought them ashore, since netting salmon was illegal.

Back in the 1970s, not long after I had moved to Powerstock, I walked up the valley past Nettlecombe, following the Mangerton Brook towards its source at the foot of Eggardon. Locals will know that beyond Castle Mill Farm there is a modest waterfall, and on the bank below it at the foot of a pool lay just such a fish, fresh from the sea and shining silver, lying dead on the bank. It had been bitten below the gills, probably by an otter, and was the length of my forearm. How it got there I had no idea, as only a mile and a quarter (two kilometres) of our local river system was accessible to spawning migratory fish at that time.

BROWN TROUT *Salmo trutta*

Since then, I have regularly patrolled the valley in the hope of spotting a sea trout, but in vain. All I have seen are small brown trout, hovering like shadows in the pools below my garden or jumping the weir when the river is high – and few of them more than 10 inches (25 centimetres) long.

But then, returning home one evening after feeding our hens, I noticed a sudden commotion in the stream, followed by the briefest glimpse of a dark polished head. My first thought was otter, or perhaps a mink; so quietly I crept along the bank and to my astonishment saw not one but two large fish in the shallows. Without a doubt they were sea trout, of a size not dissimilar to the one I had seen all those years ago, and in the throes of spawning. The female was busily excavating a hollow in the gravel in which to lay her eggs, and the cock fish was waiting to fertilise them.

In Victorian times any sea trout wanting to swim upstream would have had to run a gauntlet of pollution generated by Bridport's hemp and flax industries, to say nothing of raw sewage discharged directly into the river. Now times have changed. The waters are running cleaner again, and thanks to the fish pass installed beside Palmers Brewery in 2012, sea trout can now make their way through Bridport and on up the Symene, Asker and Mangerton to enrich our lives with their elusive presence.

OF all the night sounds to be heard in the British countryside there is nothing so chilling as the scream of a vixen. Often, waking in the small hours when the frost is fierce, I hear the hills echoing to that harsh, weird cry. How does it translate, that 'wow-wow-wow' with the last syllable hanging on the wind? Mostly, it is a contact call: 'I am here; where are you?' And in January it means love is in the air.

Foxes are mostly active at night, but once I came across a magnificent dog fox in broad daylight. His thick winter coat was a rich red-gold with a dusting of white-tipped hairs on his rump and a bold white tip to his bushy tail. I followed him unseen as he loped over the skyline. And when at last I caught up with him, to my surprise there were now four foxes chasing each other around a blackthorn thicket. I could only imagine that one of them was a vixen on heat and the others were her suitors – including the handsome dog I had seen earlier.

DEEPEST midwinter, when hoar frost lingers all day under the hedges and the ground turns to iron underfoot, is a good time to explore Powerstock Common's ancient woodlands. Otherwise, these boggy bottomlands can become a quagmire that threatens to suck the boots from your feet.

No ordinary woods, these. Wild and wolfish under a winter sky, their goblin oaks pour across the uneven ground in a writhing tide of tangled boughs. Dank and lichen-bearded, they are of the same wizened pedigree as Wistman's Wood on Dartmoor; and when the light begins to fade, they exude the same vague air of disquiet.

Why should the silence under those misshapen candelabras appear so sinister? Perhaps it is because of the looming presence of Eggardon at whose feet they lie, and the tales told by motorists coming by night over the Roman road, of phantom centurions on patrol, and the ghost of a woman who, so goes the tale, can turn up unbidden in the back seat of your car.

Powerstock Common's arboreal greybeards are a poignant reminder of the vanished oak woods that once covered most of Britain. Their ancestors stood here in King Athelstan's reign, more than a hundred years before the Norman Conquest (there is still a King's Farm at the foot of the hill). They were here even before the Romans built their road across the downs from Dorchester and may well be direct descendants of the primeval forest that emerged after the last Ice Age.

Back in the 1960s, ancient woodlands such as those on Powerstock Common were still being clear-felled by the Forestry Commission; but since then, there has been a change of heart. Today, there is a new awareness that gives such places a value beyond the balance sheet. They are our sacred groves, living records of the world about us, deeply rooted in the affections of local people, to be cherished in much the same way as we care for our parish churches.

In conservation terms their value cannot be quantified. Once destroyed, such woodlands can never be recreated, and the species they harbour – not only the fallow deer whose tracks are imprinted on every woodland path, but also the birds, lichens, fungi, insects and shade-loving plants – rely on their over-arching canopies to survive.

Apart from Ireland, ours is the most naked country in Europe. The fathomless forests of Dark Age England have gone forever – and that is why in the depths of winter, especially towards dusk in the gathering gloom, you can sometimes catch the echo of an older Britain among the deepening shadows to remind us of how much we have lost.

FEBRUARY

WHAT a joy to find snowdrops in full bloom. Of all our wild flowers they are the purest, the most ethereal, spreading in deep drifts beneath the hazels that follow the riverbanks all the way down our little valley. A sight as uplifting in their own quiet way as the return of the swallows in a few weeks' time.

How did they come here? Impossible to say. Snowdrops were not even recognised as a wild plant until the 18th century, and it is only here in the southwest that they thrive naturally in our damp winter woods and valleys. But there is no doubt that winter floods help them to spread, washing them downstream to take root in the rich waterside humus and form new colonies for our delight.

Snowdrops are not the only signs that winter's grip is loosening. Thrushes sing from the treetops, proclaiming their rights to breeding territories. Hungry gangs of long-tailed tits swing among the fattening hazel catkins, and even the iron-grey elder bushes now sport rich beetroot-coloured buds as the first lesser celandines emerge along the hedgerows. Celandines are sensitive flowers, never opening until the sun is up, closing at the merest hint of rain and shutting tight long before nightfall. Even more than the snowdrops, they herald a return to longer days as the earth begins to turn its back on winter.

EVERY year around snowdrop time, a wintry miracle takes place as common frogs emerge from hibernation and gather in shallow ponds to spawn. On windless days the soft, croaking voices of the males can be heard crooning amphibian songs of love as they embrace the females in a process known as amplexus, sometimes remaining in their amorous piggyback posture for weeks until at last, early one morning, the spawn is laid in a single spasm.

Miraculously, once they have returned to their favourite ponds, frogs can hold their breath underwater for up to seven hours by absorbing oxygen through their skin.

Each female will produce between 1,000 and 2,000 eggs, every one enclosed in its individual life-support system of jelly, forming floating masses among the water plants. Three weeks after being laid,

COMMON FROG *Rana temporaria*

the first tiny tadpoles emerge and take about 12 weeks to develop into small but perfect miniature frogs, ready to take their first leap into the dangerous world beyond the pond. There they may encounter many enemies, including herons, otters and foxes.

Add the perils of global warming, together with urbanisation, pollution and amphibian diseases such as *Ranavirus,* and no wonder frog populations are in decline, despite being protected under the Wildlife and Countryside Act of 1981.

The common toad, which usually spawns next month, faces the same dangers, and is now classified as 'seriously threatened'. Hardly surprising when it has been estimated that 20 tons (20,000 kilograms) of toads are killed on British roads every year.

With their squat bodies and warty skins, toads differ from frogs in many respects. They tend to walk rather than hop, and live away from water, hiding by day and emerging at night to feed on slugs, worms and other invertebrates. Their spawn, too, is unlike that of frogs, being laid in long strings, and their tadpoles lack the faint golden freckles that adorn those of the common frog.

MY friend Hugh Miles, the wildlife film cameraman, called in to see me today.

He lives in Corfe Mullen in East Dorset and fancied a walk, even though gales were forecast. So off we went for a brisk stroll beside the stream before lunch.

Hugh loves our West Dorset countryside. Wilder, hillier and with what he calls 'more texture' when compared with his home patch among the waterside meadows of the Stour. We talked of a summer sequel to his award-winning film, *Winter Days*, for which I had written a commentary, and thought about suitable sights and sounds:

orchids and cuckoos, sea pinks on the cliffs at Burton Bradstock, nightjars at dusk on the Arne peninsula.

How remote they all seemed on this raw February morning. But then we heard lesser redpolls calling and forgot about summer. We found them feeding in the alders with a flock of siskins and what I took to be a goldcrest, but which Hugh identified by its prominent white eyestripe as a firecrest.

We walked on. Where the stream has cut deep into the underlying sandstone its banks are steep and the water runs through miniature canyons dripping with liverworts and mosses. Small trout fled at our approach, and a grey wagtail rose from a stone where it had been bobbing in the shallows.

Of all the wagtails, the grey has the longest tail; and among the birds that remain in this valley all year round, few give me more pleasure than this restless sprite with the sulphur rump. As we drew closer it flew off downstream, a solitary fleck of glowing yellow in the cheerless winter gloom.

LET us examine the prickly subject of hedgehogs. A report published by the People's Trust for Endangered Species and the British Hedgehog Preservation Society reveals a nationwide decline in the numbers of these endearing little mammals. Twenty years ago, England's hedgehog population stood at over one million; but in the past 15 years the species has declined by half in rural areas such as ours, and by a third in urban ones.

The loss of hedgerows and intensive farming in rural areas, together with the use of pesticides and an obsession for tidy fenced-in gardens in towns and suburbs – these are just some of the threats currently hastening the demise of one of Britain's favourite animals.

EUROPEAN HEDGEHOG *Erinaceus europaeus*

Many people in West Dorset point to the badger as a major culprit. We live in a badger stronghold and there is no doubt that these voracious omnivores will eat every hedgehog they can find. Badgers are regular visitors to our garden, and I cannot remember the last time I saw a hedgehog.

But it is too simplistic to blame the badger as the main cause of their disappearance. According to the Dorset Wildlife Trust, hedgehogs are declining just as severely in areas without high badger numbers such as East Anglia, suggesting that lack of food and loss of habitat could be the driving factors.

'Removing badgers would not bring back the habitat and we would be left still struggling to keep hedgehogs surviving in areas where there is not enough food or shelter,' says the Trust.

Instead, to reverse their decline, the Dorset Mammal Group has embarked upon an extraordinary demonstration of conservation at grassroots level – namely, to transform Dorset into a hedgehog-friendly county. Inspired by a talk by the People's Trust for Endangered Species at Bridport Town Hall, the idea has spread to more than a score of self-proclaimed hedgehog-friendly towns and villages of which West Milton is one of the most recent.

As the Dorset Mammal Group likes to point out, Britain's gardens still have the potential to provide sanctuary for a wide variety of wild creatures. Indeed, added together they represent an area bigger than all our National Nature Reserves.

One way to help is to make gardens more hedgehog-friendly. This can be done by making a small hole – no bigger than a CD case – in your garden fence so that hedgehogs can move more easily from one place to another in search of shelter, food and mates. Not much to ask for an animal that will repay your kindness by gobbling up slugs and snails in return.

HOW many people do you know who own a weir? When we moved to West Milton nearly three decades ago it went with the territory, and we have lived with its water music ever since.

It was built long ago in Georgian times, to divert water from the Mangerton River down the leat to Milton Mill. There, the mill wheels have long since ceased to turn, but the leat still flows, and the weir still roars when the river is high.

At such times we watch for trout as they leap from the foam on their way to the spawning redds upstream; and when the river is quiet again, we keep an eye out for the sudden movements that betray a dipper curtseying on the lip of the weir, or the flurry of wagtails hunting for insects. And always, however seldom we are rewarded, we keep our fingers crossed for the glimpse of an otter.

It's a well-known fact that otters don't like swimming over weirs. Instead, they prefer to walk around them. So, the coping stones around the spillway are a likely spot to discover their spraints – the telltale droppings a dog otter leaves to mark his territory.

I found one earlier this month, a fresh, tarry smudge on the mossy ledges above the river. With thumb and forefinger, I could feel the thistle points of tiny fish bones, and when I gingerly gave it a sniff,

I was surprised to find it not unpleasant. Instead, it gave out its own distinctively musky odour.

As for the otter that left his fishy calling card, I never saw him. His nocturnal lifestyle makes this most elusive of hunters hard to encounter in the wild, and the modest little Mangerton itself is too small to sustain otters for long.

No wonder it is sometimes called a brook, as if river is too grand a word for a watercourse less than nine miles long. Yet it defines the adage that small is beautiful. Born in the shadow of Eggardon Hill, it dribbles out of Powerstock Common's waterlogged oak woods before flowing under the road below King's Farm to wind its way westward down to Powerstock.

By then it has already acquired its first waterfall in the valley above Nettlecombe, continuing in a succession of alder-lined pools and stony shallows to skirt Mangerton Mill, growing wider and deeper all the time until it meets the Asker at Bradpole.

It may lack the grandeur of the Severn, or the history of the Thames with its pleasure boats and rumbling bridges, but I'll settle for our own little river with its kingfishers and water crowfoot and, if very lucky, a fierce whiskered head, breaking its surface.

THE Covid crisis has demonstrated just how deadly pandemics can be – not only to us but to the plant world as well. In 1976 I wrote an obituary for the English elm which appeared in the *Sunday Times*. Less than a decade earlier, 23 million elms flourished south of a line from Birmingham to The Wash. For centuries they had soared over roadside and hedgerow, sustaining the illusion of England as a woodland country. Today they are just a memory, laid low by Dutch elm disease, an arboreal Black Death that killed every tree it infected.

ASH *Fraxinus excelsior*

Just like the plague, which arrived on the back of the black rat, Dutch elm disease also had its Trojan Horse – a small beetle with a double-barrelled name, *Scolytus scolytus*, which laid its eggs under the bark, spreading a deadly fungus in the process. No-one seems sure where the disease originated but its identity was established by the Dutch in the 1920s and the name has stuck.

Now a similar fate seems destined to overtake our ash trees. Like Covid, ash dieback originated in the Far East and is caused by a fungus against which our native ash trees have no natural protection.

According to the Woodland Trust, it will kill around 80 per cent of ash trees across the UK at a cost of billions, dramatically changing the landscape forever and threatening many species which are dependent on them. And Dorset, where the ash is a far more important component of the landscape than elm trees ever were, is bound to suffer.

Our Viking ancestors revered the ash as *Yggdrasil* – the sacred 'Tree of Life'. In February it is still dormant, its black velvet leaf buds clenched tight against the cold.

But when they open, according to country lore, we may know what kind of summer we can look forward to. 'If the oak before the ash, then we'll only get a splash; but if the ash before the oak, then we will surely get a soak!'

SPOOKY Lane is what West Milton residents call it, and not without reason. Go there at dusk and in no time you find yourself following a sunken footpath, more badger track than Queen's highway, burrowing into the surrounding hillsides.

On either side the banks rise sheer, crowned by tall trees that almost shut out the sky. Their tangled roots have created a living undercroft in which mosses flourish in the shade and hart's tongue ferns sprout from damp walls of crumbling greensand bedrock – known locally by the wonderfully evocative name of fox mould.

Welcome to the holloways of West Dorset, the spider's web of ancient byways and half-forgotten packhorse trails that came into existence long before the motor car.

They were created over the centuries by a constant procession of tramping feet, horses' hooves, and heavy, rumbling wagon wheels. Winter rains dug them even deeper, washing away the churned-up soil until today they lie as far as 30 feet (9 metres) beneath the level of the surrounding fields.

Their name is derived from the Anglo-Saxon, *hola weg*, and in West Dorset they add immeasurably to the lure of the landscape. Some of the finest examples are etched into the hills behind Symondsbury and Chideock, and feature in the pages of *Rogue Male*, Geoffrey Household's gripping thriller. Published in 1939 on the eve of World War II, this was where Household's hero evaded his Nazi pursuers by going to earth like a hunted fox in one of West Dorset's most ancient byways.

MARCH

SPRINGTIME is not far off. That is what the snowdrops told us. Having already bloomed and faded, they are now giving way to garden daffodils and other bulbs induced into flowering early by an absurdly mild February. But one of the wettest winters on record has not finished with us yet. As I write, on a rare day of blue skies and sunshine, every field is a quagmire, every brimming ditch and stream awash with muddy brown floodwater. Bad weather for humans; perfect for alder trees.

Often overlooked when compared with nobler species such as oak, beech and lime, the humble alder is the most English of trees and thrives in our wet climate. A member of the birch family, it is a pioneer species and loves to stand with its feet in the water.

Here in Dorset, it makes no great height and its timber – white when growing but a livid orange when freshly cut and exposed to the air – has little value nowadays. But always it adds shade and cover

ALDER *Alnus glutinosa*

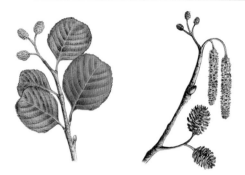

to the valley bottoms, binding the riverbanks with tangled roots. And when its catkins flower among the old year's clustered cones, the lowly alder provides a welcome moment of sombre beauty, a quiet glow of bronze and scarlet to light up the wintry hollows. You do not have to look far to find it growing abundantly on riverbanks and in soggy places, sometimes creating waterlogged jungles of a habitat known as alder carr – our very own English Everglades.

In bygone times its timber was greatly valued because it does not rot in water. Many a child would have clattered to school in clogs made of alder, and all over the country our wharves and docks were once made from it. Nor was its use confined to Britain. Some of Venice's most treasured buildings including the Rialto are propped up on alder piles, as are several of Europe's medieval cathedrals.

Alders produce male and female flowers on the same tree. Their brown-and-yellow catkins are the males, and the small cones are the females. Once fertilised they turn green, but in winter they still give out a warm glow of claret among the bare trees, and their seeds are a staple winter food for siskins.

The siskin is one of our smallest finches, like a miniature greenfinch with a distinctive forked tail. There are currently around 369 breeding pairs in Britain and in previous winters small flocks have been regular visitors to our garden bird table.

Sadly, this year not one has turned up. Perhaps they have been able to find enough wild food in the open countryside due to the unusually springlike weather.

EASILY recognised by its long black-tipped ears, the brown hare has always been a creature of mystery and superstition – hence the old English poem called 'The Creature No One Dares to Name', which describes:

The stubble-stag, the long lugs,
The stook deer, the frisky legs,
The wild one, the skipper,
The hug-the-ground, the lurker.

True spirits of the open grasslands, they are thought to have originated on the central Asian steppes and were introduced into Britain in Roman times. Being nocturnal, they spend most of the day resting in their forms (shallow depressions in the grass) and unlike rabbits they live exclusively above ground, breeding at any time from February to September and producing up to four litters a year.

When I first came to live in Dorset, I often saw them where the Roman road runs over the downs between Dorchester and Eggardon Hill. But the old sheep walks and their ancient pastures have long since been ploughed into oblivion – harebells, blue butterflies, Bronze Age barrows and all. Now, making it still harder for hares to survive, the downland fields are disappearing under alien seas of plastic, laid down to increase the maize harvest.

Few changes have wrought more visual impact to the gentle face of rural Dorset than the shift from pasture to ploughland on our rolling chalklands. In Thomas Hardy's time the downs ran in grassy crests like a rising sea before the wind, rolling from Eggardon to Cranborne Chase with hardly a blemish. Constellations of grazing sheep shone like stars on their furrowed flanks, and in summer every fold and combe was strewn with the wild flowers of the high chalk.

The greatest losses occurred between 1950 and 1980. In 1956 Dorset could boast of 44,000 acres of open country, but by 1967 nearly 10,000 acres had gone. In England as a whole, in a single decade (1960–70) a million acres went under the plough, leaving the downs laid bare down to their chalk bones, stripping away the living turf and destroying its irreplaceable communities of flowering plants, insects and birds.

Nothing was sacred – not even Sites of Special Scientific Interest, and the losses have not been confined to wildlife alone. In the past few decades Dorset has also witnessed the destruction of countless prehistoric tumuli and Celtic field systems, and the fact that it has been taking place within the Dorset AONB is even more unforgivable.

To make matters worse a deadly rabbit virus has jumped the species barrier and is now bearing down on the UK's rapidly dwindling hare population, with Dorset among the first parts of the country to be affected. Yet brown hares can still be shot at any time throughout the year and are the only game species in the UK without a closed season when hunting is prohibited. A cause for shame, you might think. The brown hare has proved itself to be a natural survivor but will need more than its uncanny alertness and astonishing turn of speed if it is to stay ahead of the disease and changing agricultural practices that are tipping the balance against it.

PATROLLING the riverbank in search of otter prints, a sudden movement catches my eye. There is no mistaking that bouncing ball of sooty feathers with a smart white bib and a rusty waistband. It is a dipper – the UK's only aquatic songbird – and it is plain to see how it got its name. Perched on a rock in midstream, it continues bobbing and curtseying as if dancing to a hidden beat, with a rhythm as regular as a metronome, until eventually it flies off downstream to continue its jive elsewhere.

But why does the dipper dip? No-one seems entirely sure. Is it a survival strategy, a movement designed to confuse any predators? Or does bobbing up and down make it easier to spot prey underwater? Most likely it is a way of communicating to other dippers, especially in the mating season. Whatever the truth, the sight of this dapper little bird never fails to lift the spirits.

What really makes dippers unique is not their distinctive movements, or even the fact that their sweet warbling song can still be heard in winter. It is their extraordinary ability to walk underwater in search of mayfly nymphs, caddis fly larvae and freshwater shrimps.

DIPPER *Cinclus cinclus*

Equally intriguing is the way the same nests are used year after year by successive generations of birds. The site itself is usually hidden in a natural bankside crevice – a mossy dome relined in spring with an inner cup of hair and rootlets in which four to five eggs are laid.

For as long as I can remember, dippers have always nested among the dripping mosses and liverworts of Milton Mill's old mill race, and it pleases me to think that the birds I see there now are the direct descendants of those whose presence so delighted the writer Kenneth Allsop when he lived there in the 1980s.

THERE'S no mistaking that rat-tat-tat sound. It is our resident great spotted woodpecker, beating a retreat for winter as he drums on the trunk of a walnut tree. Both sexes indulge in this springtime habit, but this is the male, identifiable by the prominent red patch on the back of his head.

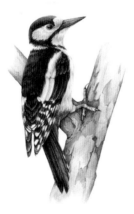

GREAT SPOTTED WOODPECKER *Dendrocopos major*

Blackbird sized, with a distinctive bouncing flight, these jaunty birds are regular garden visitors, attracted by feeders full of peanuts, sunflower seeds and other bird-table treats. But right now, they have other priorities as the breeding imperative takes over.

Great spotted woodpeckers are strongly territorial, occupying an area of about 12 acres (50,000 square metres) all year round, in which they will find a suitable tree and chisel out a new nesting hole every year. Here, next month, between four and six white glossy eggs will be laid in the safety of the hollowed-out cavity.

With 140,000 breeding pairs spread across Britain they are by far our most common woodpecker, greatly outnumbering the green woodpecker (52,000 breeding pairs) and the sparrow-sized lesser spotted woodpecker – a much less common bird with only 2,000 pairs.

Like all woodpeckers, evolution has transformed them into perfect tree climbers. With two toes pointing forwards and two pointing backwards on each foot, they can shimmy up the steepest trunks, helped by their stiff tail feathers which act as a prop. But it's those drumming skills that make the great spotted woodpecker so special – the ability to deliver up to 16 strikes a second in short, staccato bursts. And when you hear that welcome sound, you can be sure that spring is truly on its way.

🐝

MARCH is the month in which we welcome the spring equinox, the magical moment when the plane of the earth's Equator passes the centre of the sun, and daytime and night are roughly the same length.

The rites of spring are everywhere as primroses take pride of place and brimstone butterflies emerge from hibernation. Already the first chiffchaffs have arrived, leaf-thin warblers from sub-Saharan Africa, lisping their name again and again as they flit among the ash boughs.

Sadly, the dawn chorus is no longer what it used to be. For decades, the numbers of most of our songbirds have been in free fall, with turtle doves, nightingales and cuckoos among the worst-hit species. Nowadays, to be sure of hearing a cuckoo I go to the Somerset Levels; and the last place I heard a nightingale's song was five years ago on Lydlinch Common, near Sturminster Newton.

Increasingly, with global warming taking hold, as many as 1,000 chiffchaffs now stay with us all year in Britain, as do some 3,000 blackcaps, another of our most common warblers. But the overwhelming numbers of blackcaps are migrants, arriving from Germany and eastern Europe in late March. Only the males sport the eponymous black cap (the females have a rich chestnut topknot), and when you hear the male's beautiful song, you'll know why it's also known as the 'nightingale of the north'.

Other warblers have not fared so well. When I first came to live in Dorset, a pair of grasshopper warblers bred every year in the valley below Nettlecombe, and on soft spring evenings I would hear their strange, high-pitched whirring song, like an angler's reel endlessly unwinding. Now, like the house martins that once nested under the eaves of the Three Horseshoes in Powerstock, they are just a memory.

EVEN before the summer visitors turn up, our bird table is as busy as ever with goldfinches, bullfinches, great tits and blue tits, although the gang of long-tailed tits that graced our garden for weeks have now dispersed, presumably to pair off and breed.

But we are still not yet out of the woods. Dormice know that, and remain curled up tight, hibernating in their winter nests among tree roots and coppiced hazels until April. For this is the time of the blackthorn winter when snow-white blossom smothers the hedgerows.

Blackthorn is widespread in Dorset. Although seldom growing more than 12 feet (three and a half metres) tall, it is a common hedgerow tree which also creates impenetrable thickets on parts of Powerstock Common. Its Latin name, *Prunus spinosa*, refers to its wicked thorns, and the white flowers that emerge before it puts out its leaves will eventually become the grape-blue sloes of autumn.

When at last the leaves appear, they are a precious food plant for a host of insects, including the larvae of magpie moths and the elusive brown hairstreak butterfly. Then comes my favourite day of the year when the clocks go forward, heralding the season of long, light evenings and the return of the swallows and other spring migrants.

WHAT a wily bird is the woodcock. Shy and secretive, essentially crepuscular, the 'snipe of the woods' is a master of disguise. Its cryptic plumage is the colour of dead bracken and the old year's leaves. A perfect camouflage as it hides in the woods, waiting for darkness.

WOODCOCK *Scolopax rusticola*

33

Only if disturbed will it explode from the woodland floor and then zigzag away through the trees. But with the coming of spring, you may be lucky enough to see woodcock flitting like souls through the gathering dusk as the males perform their mysterious breeding display flights – a unique behaviour known as 'roding.'

Alas, Britain's share of the world's woodcock population is falling fast. Although more than 55,000 pairs still breed here, their numbers have declined by 50 per cent over the last 25 years, causing the RSPB to place the woodcock on their Red List of threatened species.

In the circumstances I find it disappointing to discover these exquisite waders are still considered fair game by the shooting community, for whom the woodcock's jinking flight represents the ultimate test in target practice.

The Game & Wildlife Conservation Trust reckons that over 90 per cent of all woodcocks shot in Britain belong to the 1.4 million overwintering birds that migrate from as far away as Russia, where numbers are stable. But critics – among them the BBC's *Springwatch* presenter Chris Packham – argue that if a species is in decline, you should not shoot it. Unsurprisingly, his broadside did not go down well with those who only view nature down the barrel of a gun.

The country sports lobby paints a positive picture of the undeniable benefits of game shooting and its value to the economy in terms of cash and jobs. But when it comes to woodcocks, I am with Packham. In this case it really is time for the shooting lobby to show some voluntary restraint; and if that does not work then statutory restriction is the only solution.

THE red berries of winter are long gone, stripped bare by hungry flocks of fieldfares. Now, encouraged by the lengthening days, a mist

BRIMSTONE *Gonepteryx rhamni*

of green runs through the hedgerows as the hawthorns burst into leaf. The first brimstone butterflies are on the wing, and already the sheltered hedge-bank primroses are turning their faces to the sun.

Britain is blessed with some 28,000 miles of hedgerows and each one is precious, an entire ecosystem in miniature, an unofficial nature reserve offering refuge for innumerable species of wild plants and creatures that could not survive in open country.

Some were established as windbreaks or barriers to prevent livestock from straying. Others mark old boundaries and rights of way, and among the oldest are the ghosts of forgotten forests, created by our forefathers as they hewed their homesteads from the primeval wildwood. The oldest date from the Bronze Age and the custom of laying down stock-proof barriers was continued, first by the Romans and then the Saxons. Even the word hedge itself is derived from the Old English *hecg*, meaning an enclosure.

The older the hedge, the more likely it is to have a greater variety of trees and shrubs, and there is a good rough-and-ready way of estimating its age. Simply count how many different species – such as hawthorn, blackthorn, hazel, ash, oak, holly, crab apple, spindle and field maple – can be found in a 100-foot (30-metre) length and allow 100 years for each one. This is the 'hedgerow hypothesis' devised in the 1970s by Dr Max Hooper, the eminent plant ecologist; and if he is right, it means that many of the hedges around Powerstock must have stood here since the Conquest.

Yet regardless of age and their value in defining sense of place, hedgerows are the most important wildlife habitat for most of our lowland countryside. No less than 21 of our 28 lowland mammals depend on them, not only the hedgehog, dormouse, harvest mouse and bank vole, but also the stoats and weasels that prey on them; and according to the RSPB at least 30 bird species build their nests in hedgerows, among them blackbirds, song thrushes, lesser whitethroats, yellowhammers, linnets and dunnocks.

By the time the Enclosure Acts of the mid-18th century had laid their rectilinear hedges across the open common lands, the quintessential chequerboard landscape of the British countryside was complete. And in West Dorset, especially at Kingcombe and in the lush bottomlands of the Marshwood Vale, the living mosaic of old meadows and their hedgerows defines the character of the landscape.

In my lifetime Britain has lost more than half a million miles of hedgerows in the relentless drive for more efficient farming. Yet, managed by hand in the old manner, cutting and trimming just once in a decade, there is no reason why a hedge should not continue to harbour its rabbits, wild flowers and dunnocks' nests for another thousand years.

❧

IT is not often that you happen upon an act of murder in Dorset. The victim, a song thrush, lay on its back in the lane. The assailant, a male sparrowhawk, crouched over it like the villain in a Victorian melodrama, its wings spread wide to conceal the crime.

Caught red-handed, he made no move to escape but stood his ground, a furious bundle of pent-up energy glaring at me with burning eyes as if daring me to come closer.

Of all our British birds of prey, none cuts such a rakish dash as the sparrowhawk with its barred chest and blue-grey mantle. It is the hedgerow assassin, a killer not much bigger than the birds it terrorises, possessing a deceptively lethal power in its spindly yellow shanks.

It was easy to reconstruct the crime. When I lived in Powerstock a pair of sparrowhawks nested just below my cottage in the fork of an old crab apple. I often saw the male, quartering the valley on his regular hunting forays; and the female, too, a bigger, browner bird, skimming down the lanes barely a foot above the tarmac.

Once I caught her pluming a wood pigeon nearly twice her size; but pigeons were too big for the male to tackle. Dunnocks and finches were his favourites and his method of hunting them was unerringly effective. First, he would circle, gaining height. Then, like a wartime Spitfire coming out of the sun, he would slant across the fields in a fast hedge-hopping dive to grab whatever unsuspecting target happened to be on the other side.

Back in the 1960s the sparrowhawk was almost wiped out by pesticides. Then the poisons were banned, and the hawks bounced back. It may be tough on the thrushes and finches, but the sight of a sparrowhawk on patrol is a sure sign that the land is healing, fit to live in again, not just for hawks but for humans, too.

APRIL

HOW quickly the year is slipping past. Only yesterday we were admiring the first snowdrops. Now they are just a memory as spring truly hits its stride and a frenzy of cheerful, twittering voices ring out from the roadside telephone wires, announcing the return of the swallows that nest in our log shed.

Gilbert White, the 18th-century parson-naturalist, thought they spent the winter hibernating in the mud of village ponds; but the truth is even more extraordinary – how a bird weighing less than one ounce (28 grams) makes a 12,000-mile (20,000-kilometre) round trip every year between Dorset and southern Africa.

Most of our Dorset birds spend the winter in the reed beds near Bloemfontein, as the writer Horatio Clare lyrically describes in his book, *A Single Swallow*. To return to the savannahs beyond the Sahel – not only the adults but juveniles making the journey for the first time – they migrate by day, flying low so they can feed on their way.

SWALLOW *Hirundo rustica*

Southward they swarm over the English Channel, covering 200 miles (320 kilometres) a day at speeds of anything up to 35 miles an hour (56 kilometres an hour), pouring through western France and skirting the great barrier of the Pyrenees before crossing the Mediterranean to Morocco and the sub-Saharan lands beyond.

Often, I have watched them in Africa, swooping among the Serengeti wildebeest herds in the company of other European migrants, including white storks born on the church towers of Portugal and southern Spain. Living in Britain as we do, it is only natural to think of these swallows as ours, when in fact they belong just as much to their wintering grounds south of the Equator.

Their autumn migration takes around four months, but the return journey is much faster, driven by the breeding imperative. Many will die from starvation and exhaustion. Storms take their toll, as do birds of prey such as the hobby, the dashing little falcon that also returns to our shores in the spring. But the great majority will survive to complete their journey home in five weeks and delight us again with their joyful presence.

LONG before the Romans settled in Dorchester another race of empire builders was silently colonising the West Dorset hillsides. *Lasius flavus* is the Latin name for the yellow meadow ant whose distinctive mounds are a classic feature of unploughed grassland. Each mound is an underground metropolis, a home for up to 14,000 ants, and some of their grassy hummocks could be centuries old.

They are easy to see if you follow the Ant Hill Trail, the four-mile (six-kilometre) waymarked route that snakes through the valleys around West Milton. Developed by the Dorset Wildlife Trust, the Grasslands Trust and the Kingcombe Visitor Centre, the walk takes in two of the Trust's reserves at South Poorton and Loscombe.

One of the Trail's finest stretches leads out of West Milton into what locals call the Secret Valley, where a trickling stream finds its way down from Poorton through a boggy jungle in which marsh marigolds shine among the alders.

The Trail clings to the steep valley sides where bluebells flourish among the bracken and fallow deer are commonly seen; and apart from an occasional field gate or barbed wire fence there is nothing to tell you what century you are in.

Until now. On a recent walk I watched a buzzard drift overhead and followed its progress over the medieval lynchets that climb in seven giant steps up the opposite side of the valley. And as I did so I noticed for the first time the distant outline of Powerstock's new mobile phone mast on the skyline.

By no amount of exaggeration could one describe it as conspicuous. Nor can you see it for more than a couple of hundred yards as you follow the Trail out of the village. Nevertheless its very presence overlooking this timeless combe feels like an unwelcome intrusion, proclaiming the arrival of the 21st century.

WHEN was the last time you heard a cuckoo? Every April without fail its unmistakeable two-note call would echo among the listening hillsides, announcing the arrival of the Dorset spring. But that was back in the days when grasshopper warblers still lit up the valley below with their strange, reeling song at dusk. Nowadays if you want to hear cuckoos you need to travel as far as the Somerset Levels to hear their haunting woodwind voices.

But not all is lost. Rachel Carson's fearful vision of a silent spring has not yet overtaken us, and the dawn chorus, at least here in West Dorset, is still a source of wonder as it spills down the valley from Eggardon and washes across the meadows.

Awake at first light with the windows wide open, I unravel the early morning soundtrack, mentally ticking off the individual contributors: song thrush, mistle thrush, wheezing greenfinches, male chaffinches in full cry, and wrens with voices far bigger than their diminutive bodies. Green woodpeckers add occasional peals of laughter and wood pigeons chant the same deep chorus, over and over in the background.

But the blackbird is my favourite songster. Always has been since I first listened to its throaty contralto in the side-by-side gardens of the Surrey suburbs where I grew up. More poignant to me than any nightingale, a blackbird singing from an apple tree summons up the essence of the English spring. Yet, whenever thinking of the springtime soundtrack that plays across our rural parish, it is not the blackbird's rich contralto that first comes to mind. It is the constant cawing of rooks, a noise as timeless as the countryside itself.

Since time immemorial, theirs has been one of the defining sounds of the English countryside, and the birds themselves are a common sight as they come together in large flocks, sometimes in the company of jackdaws. Not so many years have passed since rook pie was a popular seasonal staple in rural areas, but the species has continued to thrive and multiply.

BLACKBIRD *Turdus merula*

They are among the most faithful of birds, forming pair bonds that last a lifetime. Like all members of the crow family, they are highly intelligent and have been known to use tools and solve problems. Today, we have something like one million breeding pairs in Britain and no sign of their numbers declining. Their sociable nature is one way to tell them apart from the more solitary carrion crows, hence the old saying: 'A rook on its own is a crow'. But their most defining feature is the bare white mask at the base of the beak.

The rooks were already nest-building when the snowdrops were in flower, and for weeks now, their harsh clamour has become our village evensong as they circle overhead before roosting in the trees near Milton Mill.

From my office window I can see them as I write, blown about the sky like scraps of burnt paper. Their untidy stick-pile nests are built from twigs snapped off living trees and seldom picked up from the ground, although they are not averse to stealing from their neighbours.

Eggs laid in early March have hatched, and the rookery is now at its busiest as both parents fly in and out with food – mostly worms and insect larvae – to feed their noisy fledglings. At times, the noise is deafening. No wonder they are known collectively as a parliament of rooks!

Looking up at the tallest treetops I watch them swaying in the wind and wonder if they feel the same sensation as I once did after having climbed to the top of a tall ship as it ploughed its way around Land's End in a force eight gale! Yet however flimsy they appear, the nests and their scrawny youngsters survive.

All over the parish the same miracle of birth and renewal is taking place as birds of every species take advantage of the lengthening days to reproduce. The nests themselves vary hugely. A peregrine's eyrie is little more than a scrape on a sandstone cliff ledge, while other birds such as long-tailed tits weave fragile domes of moss and grass and cobweb strands in which to raise their young.

As for the eggs themselves, none compares with those of the song thrush. How well I remember searching for them, finding the mud-lined nest in a hawthorn bush, and dipping into it with arm outstretched to find a cluster of jewels bluer than the sky, stippled with delicate black spots.

Of course, that was when I was a boy and collecting birds' eggs was not yet illegal.

My hunting ground was Nonsuch Park in Surrey, and my friends and I knew every nest in every hedgerow, field and spinney – from the woodpecker holes in the hollow oaks to the wood pigeons' fragile rafts of twigs in the swaying tops of the pine trees.

Yet even then, we followed an unwritten code of honour, never taking an egg unless it held at least a clutch of four. And heaven help the boys we found who broke the rule!

For us it was a rite of spring, as was the art of dipping for tadpoles, or catching the first brimstone butterfly. And out of those innocent childhood pastimes grew the passion for nature that has stayed with me to this day.

THE vanishing cuckoo is not the only change to have overtaken the countryside. Even in recent years, I could never cross a meadow without rabbits' ears popping up from the long grass, or the sight of bobbing white tails disappearing in all directions as they made a dash for the safety of their hedgerow burrows. But not anymore. Today the fields stand empty, and West Dorset is a lonelier place without them.

The humble rabbit has a long history in Britain. Wiped out by the Ice Age, it was briefly replaced during Roman times but only became truly established when reintroduced by the Normans, who bred them for their meat and fur. For evidence of their popularity in the 12th century you need look no further than Coneygar Hill in Bridport, which derives its name from 'Coney Garth' – the medieval term for a commercial rabbit warren.

Inevitably, some individuals burrowed their way to freedom and quickly spread to all corners of the country. So successful were they that by the 1950s their numbers had reached 100 million – only to fall prey to myxomatosis and, more recently, an even nastier plague known as rabbit haemorrhagic disease (RHD).

RABBIT *Oryctolagus cuniculus*

Even before the scourge of myxomatosis arrived, rabbits had to go flat out to avoid a host of hungry predators such as foxes, stoats and buzzards. Although lacking the hare's turn of pace, a startled rabbit is no slouch when it comes to speed and can still clock up a decent 18 miles an hour (29 kilometres an hour) to avoid becoming a fox's dinner.

Rabbits are also blessed with something close to 360-degree vision; but their best defence mechanism is simply to go to ground. Apart from their favourite feeding times at first and last light, this is where they spend most of their lives, and where the does produce their young, giving birth to anything up to eight litters a year.

With each litter containing as many as 14 babies, one can only hope the rabbits' legendary powers of reproduction will eventually allow them to stage a welcome return to our depleted countryside.

NOW is the time to rekindle our love affair with Britain's most famous wild flower.

Bluebells spend most of their life underground as bulbs. But when April comes, their drooping stems burst forth everywhere, from the

BLUEBELL *Hyacinthoides non-scripta*

glens of Scotland to the bracken-covered clifftops of Dorset's Jurassic Coast, spreading in a violet haze through every patch of ancient woodland and anaesthetising the air with their distinctive fragrance.

They are found all over Atlantic Europe, but the UK is a bluebell stronghold, also known in other parts of the country by names such as wild hyacinth, cuckoo's boots, granfer griggles and witches' thimbles.

Since they thrive in partial shade on damp but well-drained soil, they do well in our West Dorset combes, spreading among Lewesdon's lofty beech woods, pouring through Powerstock Common's oak-wood glades and spilling down every tangled lane and hedgerow between Eggardon Hill and the Marshwood Vale.

In Victorian times bluebells were a popular symbol of everlasting love and today they are protected under the 1981 Wildlife and Countryside Act, which forbids the digging up of bulbs and all commercial harvesting.

Surprisingly, for such a lovely flower, bluebells contain toxic glycosides and are therefore harmful to people and to animals if ingested. But maybe that is just as well, for bluebells face all kinds of threats, from habitat loss to climate change. Even their own kind is a menace in the unwelcome presence of the Spanish bluebell – an alien species introduced from the Iberian peninsula. Identified by their erect stems and total lack of smell, they have jumped over the garden wall to hybridise with our native flowers in the wild.

DOWN by the sea between West Bay and Lyme Regis, the crumbling cliffs are full of fossils, as plentiful as currants in a Christmas pudding. This entire stretch of Dorset's Jurassic Coast is stuffed with them, a giant geological layer cake beginning with dark and sinister Black Ven marls, followed in turn by belemnite marls and green ammonite beds topped with a tawny spectrum of younger loams and sandstones. But the bargain basement underpinning this whole fantastic crosscut through prehistoric time is the famous Blue Lias, the graveyard of the great marine reptiles of the Jurassic world.

These blue-grey slabs of banded limestone are the oldest rocks in Dorset, and when you walk on them, as you can below the cliffs of Black Ven, you are treading on a prehistoric floor laid down by the sediment of vanished seas in which most of England lay immersed 180 million years ago.

Back then, the warm Jurassic waters swarmed with wildlife of a very different kind.

Ammonites and squid-like belemnites crawled and swam in their millions among the sea-lily meadows. Barrel-bodied plesiosaurs raised their long necks above the waves. Fierce ichthyosaurs and sea crocodiles surged through the shallows in pursuit of primeval fish and turtles. A horror-comic monster called megalosaurus roamed the marshy deltas while nightmarish pterosaurs with tooth-armoured beaks sailed overhead on leathery wings.

When they died, they sank to the bottom, there to vanish beneath the ceaseless drizzle of blue-grey sediment. And there they remain, buried under the weight of ages – teeth, scales, shells and bones – the charnel house of an entire epoch preserved and hidden beneath the Jurassic Coast until one day a chunk of cliff gives way, and the sharp tap of a fossil hunter's hammer splits open a limestone nodule and lets in the sunlight of the 21st century.

❦

EARLY morning. The dawn chorus in full swing, and a sudden blue flash catches my eye, whirring away downriver. Why does the occasional sight of a kingfisher fill me with such joy? Perhaps it is

KINGFISHER *Alcedo atthis*

because so many of our simple pleasures are rooted in childhood when everything is new and exciting.

I grew up near Ewell, in Surrey, where springs bubble out of the chalk, creating a chain of village ponds whose gin-clear waters teemed with sticklebacks. The fish in turn attracted a pair of kingfishers, and the first time I spotted them I could not believe such living jewels could exist in London's outermost suburbs.

Since then, I have seen kingfishers all over the world. Africa alone has 15 different species including the giant kingfisher, a bird the size of a bantam. But my favourite is still our own diminutive kingfisher. Measuring less than 7 inches (18 centimetres) from turquoise crown to stumpy tail, it occurs on every river in Dorset, diving into the water to catch dragonfly larvae, water beetles and small fish, which are beaten to death against a branch before being swallowed head first.

Kingfishers are highly territorial, requiring at least 1,000 yards (a kilometre) of river in which to catch 60 per cent of their body weight each day. They are also constantly alert, making it difficult to creep up on them when perched on an overhanging branch. That is why the first moment you are aware of their presence is when you hear their sharp high-pitched whistle, followed by an electric-blue spark rapidly disappearing downstream.

In April, along with many other birds, their breeding season is in full swing. Having excavated a tunnel in the riverbank, up to six glossy white eggs are laid in the nesting chamber. Both parents take it in turns to incubate and the eggs will hatch 20 days later after which the chicks stay in the nest for another 24 days.

BORN into a famous seagoing family, Victor Crutchley has kept his feet on the ground, pursuing a career in woodland management around his home in West Dorset at the foot of Eggardon. There, on a perfect afternoon on the last day of April, I joined him on a guided walk around Knowle Hill Wood, deep in the heart of the Crutchley family estate.

Once inside the wood, the tall trees closed around us, creating a silence broken only by distant snatches of birdsong and filtering out the sun whose dappled light fell across rich mauve and white carpets of bluebells and ramsons. Victor appeared to know every tree, treating them all like old friends, which was hardly surprising as he had planted so many of them himself. Among them, reaching for the sky, rose a particularly splendid specimen – a towering balsam poplar. 'The same species that once provided the arrows for the bowmen of the *Mary Rose*,' said Victor.

Other trees, notably the gnarled and crooked oaks, looked as if they had stood there forever and were clearly of the same centuries-old lineage as those of Powerstock Common, on the far side of Eggardon. And if proof were needed, it was here in the form of uncommon wild flowers such as herb Paris and twayblade – classic indicator species whose presence confirms the authenticity of ancient woodlands.

Everywhere, nature flourished unchecked. All around us, trees and dead branches had been left to lie where they fell on the forest floor, to rot and return their goodness to the earth in the natural scheme of things, reminding me of the timeless woodlands of Zambia's Luangwa River valley.

We walked on, making our way through shoulder-high jungles of pendulous sedge along deer tracks that led us ever deeper into the wood. At one point we emerged above a steep and winding *gwyle* – the Dorset dialect word for a gully – carved through the trees by a tumbling stream.

And finally, the high point of the walk, literally and metaphorically, as we zigzagged our way to the summit of Knowle Hill through a derelict hazel coppice. The sweet scent of the bluebells hung in the air, and I could see the flattened outlines of crushed flowers where fallow deer had rested during the morning. As for the coppiced hazels themselves, some were over 70 years old, said Victor, and were by far the biggest I have ever seen.

MAY

EVERY year they turn up, regular as clockwork. On the third day of May, if the weather is fine, I look up and hear them screaming overhead on flickering switchblade wings. 'They're back,' wrote the poet Ted Hughes in his exultant tribute to the swifts' return from Africa. 'They've made it again, which means the globe's still working.'

Coinciding with the beginning of summer, their arrival is a reaffirmation of the turning year and its miraculous powers of renewal, and to watch them racing overhead, carving elegant parabolas in the sky, is to recognise the inequality of our own earthbound existence.

What extraordinary creatures they are. The only birds known to mate on the wing. When a swiftlet leaves the nest, it spends the next three years of its life in the sky, hunting for insects up in the air and even sleeping above the clouds.

In appearance, swifts resemble swallows but are bigger, darker and altogether faster, fizzing over our village rooftops at speeds of 130 miles an hour (210 kilometres an hour) or more. With such mastery of the air, it is not surprising to discover they can complete their 3,000-mile (5,000-kilometre) migration from the rainforests of the Democratic Republic of the Congo in under a week.

The world population of common swifts currently stands at around 25 million birds, of which 87,000 pairs breed in Britain; but pesticides and habitat destruction take their toll, as do modern building regulations that deny the roof spaces they need for nesting. So, enjoy their fleeting presence while you can; until one day in August when you wake up to find they are gone as mysteriously as they arrived, hurtling south on their ancestral flyways back to sub-Saharan Africa.

WE leave the car in the middle of Powerstock, where five lanes meet beneath the churchyard wall. Here, surrounded by leaning headstones, stands the Church of St Mary with its crooked Norman chancel arch. Above us, gargoyles grin from the Hamstone tower and its gilded weathercock swings in the blue, pinpointing the secret heartland of a magic circle – just a few miles in diameter – that holds the essence of West Dorset.

To find unspoilt countryside half as good as this you would have to travel at least as far as Normandy, whose lush green fields and apple blossom valleys bear an uncanny resemblance to our own cider lands. Look at a map and you'll see how the contours squeeze together, marking deep, buzzard-haunted combes and sudden green hills that seem to inflate before your eyes. It's a landscape altogether too rounded and rumpled to farm intensively, and that has been its salvation.

Within minutes of leaving the village we dive off-road down a muddy lane – more badger track than rural byway – tunnelling between bluebell banks and derelict cider orchards with the tang of wild garlic all around us, and come to the green mound of a motte-and-bailey castle. To the villagers it has always been known as Humpy Castle, but legend says it stands on the site of a Saxon mead-hall built by Athelstan, the first king of all England.

Of late, the papers have been full of doom, of chronic overpopulation and the world bursting at the seams, but there is no sign of it here. No sound, either, except for blackbird song and cawing rooks, and the plaintive bleat of newborn lambs.

Ahead looms Eggardon and the Belstone Ledge, its limestone prow on which bale fires were lit in pagan times. Here we stop to catch our breath and, looking back the way we came, I can see the whole of West Dorset spread out at my feet; a sea of green broken by white-crested waves of blackthorn blossom, with Lyme Bay shining to the south and the twin hills of Lewesdon and Pilsdon Pen rising out of the Marshwood Vale.

UP early to make the most of a perfect May morning. Sun shining from a cloudless sky, and Dorset dressed in a hundred shades of green. The paddock where our Exmoor pony roams has disappeared under a carpet of buttercups and the orchard is full of cuckoo flowers.

I sit on a log by the river to watch the natural world go by, surrounded by a bankside profusion of bluebells, wild garlic, red campion and yellow dead-nettle. After a month with very little rain, the water is much lower than usual, but every pool now holds at least one trout, creating perfect circular ripples every time they rise to feed.

From the beech tree canopy above my head comes the deep-throated cooing of amorous wood pigeons. Somewhere further off a blackbird sings, and it takes only the lightest breeze to shake down the blossom from the wild cherry tree like confetti.

The sun is warmer now, and my mind begins to fill with the details of chores to be done, when a sudden movement catches my eye. It is a wild duck, a female mallard, proudly introducing her brood of eight fluffy ducklings. I knew there was a nest somewhere under the bankside alders, but this is the first time I have seen the family together proud mother and offspring in line astern.

It is a joyous moment. Not all will survive. That is why there are so many. But I wish them well as they go on their way, eagerly dabbling after floating insects with their mother fussing around them as the entire flotilla disappears around the bend on their way to Milton Mill.

IT isn't every evening that you are invited to meet a barn owl. 'Be there at eight,' said Chuck Willmott. 'That's the time he's been emerging.' According to Chuck, who lives at Bell Cottage in the back lanes between Loders and West Milton, Barny and Olive, his mate, took up residence there in March, occupying the nest box Chuck installed above the disused limekiln at the back of his garden.

Barn owls regularly nested there in the mid-1960s. So, for a while, did a pair of little owls. But when the barn owls disappeared for a time, Chuck built the box and successfully persuaded them to return last year. 'I'm not sure if it is the same pair as last year,' he said, 'but I wish them happy hunting and a successful breeding season.'

Making myself as inconspicuous as possible, I stand close to the hedge by the road and wait. The sky is overcast, with a hint of mist over Way's Hill and not a breath of wind.

I look at my watch. Eight o'clock has been and gone. On the hillside above me a roe deer steps out of the gorse and begins to feed. Then suddenly, only minutes later, an owl emerges from the nest box and flies across the meadow to alight on a fence post, staying long enough

for me to marvel at his heart-shaped facial mask, the oriental almond eyes and the pearly-king spangles on his buff-mantled shoulders.

No wonder the barn owl has always been one of my favourite birds – a ghostly hunter designed for dusk – and I relish the sight of Barny in action, wavering over the unshorn meadows on thistledown wings, pouncing on voles to feed his family of six young owlets in Chuck's nest box.

DOWN in the orchard, framed in apple blossom, a male blackbird sings his heart out.

What better time, what better place to celebrate the month of May? Traditional orchards are rarer now, and the statistics make sorry reading. Two-thirds of Britain's orchards have disappeared since 1960, but Common Ground, the Dorset-based conservation charity established in 1983, has been fighting to reverse the trend.

'Old orchards represent our best relations with nature,' says Sue Clifford who, together with co-founders Angela King and the writer Roger Deakin, came to their rescue in 1989 by launching the 'Save Our Orchards' campaign. That year they commissioned James Ravilious to document the West Country's orchards, and in 1993 they published the *Apple Map of Britain*, a stunning poster featuring over 300 traditional apple varieties, followed in 2000 with *The Common Ground Book of Orchards*, containing a positive survival plan for orchards in which everyone can participate.

For cider makers and cider drinkers their importance is a given. It was probably the Norman monks of Loders who introduced the art of cider making to our corner of West Dorset – the mysterious alchemy that transforms crushed apples into liquid gold as clear as sunlight. But for ecologists and country lovers it is the old orchards themselves that are revered as wildlife habitats. To naturalists, an ancient orchard is a treasure house of genetic diversity, a wood and meadow all in one, offering sanctuary to all kinds of creatures, from dormice to beetles.

The oldest trees may have stood here for generations. All winter long they sleep like the dead, while treecreepers run over their lichened flanks, winkling spiders from their bark. But every spring the sap still rises, and the buds burst forth, providing the fruit to fill the wassail bowl and gather once more to celebrate the turning year.

Yet wherever orchards occur their value stretches far beyond the harvest of apples and pears they produce. For every old-fashioned orchard is also a nature reserve in miniature, an eco-friendly haven for all manner of wild plants and creatures. And the older the trees the richer they are. Many are festooned with mistletoe. Little owls use holes and cavities enlarged by green and great spotted woodpeckers and bats hunt around the treetops, feasting on the wealth of insects that depend on the unshorn grass beneath while badgers and roe deer emerge at dusk to wander down their crooked aisles.

Later, when the apples ripen, most will rot where they fall, providing thrushes and hedgehogs with food for free. But now, when orange tip butterflies flip through the dappled light, when the blackbirds call and the petals drift down like falling snow, is the loveliest time of all.

Since I first came to live in West Milton, most of our old orchards have been grubbed up; but all is not lost. With traditional cider making currently enjoying a welcome renaissance there is time to cling onto the survivors, not just for the drink but also for the wildlife that flourishes under their boughs.

THIS is a tale about beauty and the beast, both of which inhabit our West Dorset streams and rivers. The beauty is the demoiselle dragonfly that appears in May, fluttering over the water on iridescent wings (indigo if male, bronze if female).

At rest, settled on a waterside reed stem, they fold their wings along the length of their slender bodies, unlike larger dragonflies whose wings are held permanently outstretched.

BANDED DEMOISELLE *Calopteryx splendens*

The beast is the brook lamprey, a sinister denizen of the riverbed. Measuring no more than 9 inches (23 centimetres) in length, lampreys are not easy to see. Just as well, probably, because lampreys are not a pretty sight.

Living leftovers from the days when the world was young, these prehistoric relics were swimming around 200 million years before the dinosaurs, and in all that time they have hardly changed. On top of their head is a single nostril. For want of gills they have seven holes behind each eye, and instead of a mouth, nature has provided them with a circular sucker armed with rasp-like teeth. Other fish are their prey, and once attached to them they suck out their juices before discarding their victim like an empty paper bag.

They take five years to mature and in May the adults gather in writhing shoals to spawn, each female depositing up to 1,200 eggs in the gravel bed after which, their life's purpose completed, they die.

Despite their unattractive appearance they were once considered a great delicacy, as were river lampreys, their much larger relatives. In the 18th century they were caught in the Thames in the tens of thousands, and were so popular in medieval times that King Henry I is said to have died after gorging on a surfeit of lampreys.

❦

IF I were an exile pining for England, then May is the month I would miss the most, when the returning swifts herald the start of summer and hawthorn blossom breaks like Atlantic surf along the hedgerows.

Throughout the parish new life is emerging. In West Milton, the blackbirds are singing fit to burst. Further afield in the surrounding combes the fallow deer are hiding their fawns, and in the wet valley bottoms where the cuckoo flowers grow is the uplifting sight of orange tip butterflies on the wing.

Only the male has those intense Day-Glo orange tips to its forewings, but both sexes share the same delicate hind-wing markings whose speckled undersides are a perfect match for the green-and-white froth of cow parsley that chokes our lanes at this time of year. Yet despite the orange tip's exquisite beauty, the month belongs to an altogether more delicate creature.

Meet the mayfly, the largest of the *Ephemeroptera* – aquatic insects with gossamer wings like miniature leaded windows. From the tip of its head to the end of its triple-whiskered tail it measures almost two inches (five centimetres) long and at rest, clinging to the underside of a leaf, its wings are pressed together like hands in prayer above the slender body.

Having spent the first two years of its life as an underwater nymph it emerges around the 15th of the month and takes to the air, rising and falling with clouds of others all caught up in the throes of their mating dance.

But true to their generic name, mayflies lead ephemeral lives. Two or three days at most and they are done. Once mated, the females return to the water to lay their eggs and die – to be gobbled up by the eagerly awaiting trout with a faint but audible smack of the lips. No wonder their sudden abundance gave rise to the phrase 'duffer's fortnight', when trout are easier to catch.

JUNE

IT was Liz Somerville's Art Week exhibition that lured me back to North Eggardon Farm. It isn't every day that you can enjoy such a comprehensive display by an artist whose highly personalised style of printmaking captures the unique spirit of the Dorset landscape.

Nor was this the only reward for heading up the single-track road beyond Nettlecombe. On either side of the tarmac rose mighty specimens of English oak, giving way eventually to nothing less than a living version of the Field of the Cloth of Gold – the summit meeting between Henry VIII and King Francis I of France that took place in a valley south of Calais. The name arose from the ostentatious arrays of golden tents and pavilions. But what now lay before me was simply a solid gold field of buttercups stretching all the way to Eggardon.

Through the middle of the field ran a grassy track, leading to the foot of the hill, and at the far end a sudden movement caught my eye. Roe deer? No. A fox perhaps? No.

I reached for my binoculars and knew what it was straight away. Those long, black-tipped lugs gave the game away. It was a brown hare, a sight seldom seen these days, and therefore all the better for it.

As I watched, it began to come closer, leisurely lolloping over the grass towards the spot where we had parked the car by the roadside. Closer it came, and closer still, until at the last moment it realised it was being watched and vanished into the buttercups. Of such magic moments are our summers made.

THE path to the clifftops runs out through fields wrapped around by wind-bent thorns. This westerly stretch of the Jurassic Coast between Lyme Regis and Burton Bradstock is inherently unstable, forever falling away in colossal landslips. Never a year passes without another huge chunk of those famous cliffs sliding into the sea.

Apart from one prominent sandstone prow, that is, whose bony ribs provide nesting sites for gulls, ravens – and peregrines.

PEREGRINE FALCON *Falco peregrinus*

From here on Thorncombe Beacon, where fires were lit to warn of the coming of the Spanish Armada, the views across Lyme Bay are stunning. On a clear day you can see Berry Head, 40 miles (65 kilometres) away in Devon, and in the opposite direction, the low-lying snout of Portland Bill sliding into the English Channel.

With binoculars I scour the cliffs' furrowed faces, looking for telltale signs of peregrines in residence. Their hunting perches are splashed with white droppings, but where are the birds themselves?

Then suddenly, floating up from the abyss, more insistent than the wailing gulls, louder than the shrilling jackdaws, comes a harsh, heckling cry that lifts the hairs on the back of my neck.

Moments later I see him. It is the tiercel, the male peregrine, so called because he is roughly one-third smaller than his mate. On switchblade wings he comes soaring past, observing me with lustrous eyes eight times more powerful than my own.

Casting around in search of a thermal he begins to ring up into the sky, effortlessly carving wide parabolas as if revelling in the sheer joy of flight until he is a mere black star beneath the clouds.

In the 1950s it seemed as if the peregrine was doomed when DDT and other pesticides caused a massive population crash. But when the poisons were banned in the early 1970s these beautiful falcons bounced back. Today they are now so numerous that some have even become city dwellers, as much at home on cathedral ledges as on West Dorset's Heritage Coast.

Mating takes place at the beginning of March. The first eggs are laid in early April and the fledglings grow fast. Any day now they will make their first laborious attempts at flight, but another six weeks will pass before they can hunt for themselves.

Now the tiercel is aloft again, and this time the female is with him. Moments later, she returns to the eyrie, but her mate is still in full flight. Riding the torrents of air flung up by the cliffs, he climbs

1,000 feet (300 metres) in a matter of seconds, then folds his wings and drops like a stone, the fastest feathered thing on earth, capable of speeds beyond 200 miles an hour (320 kilometres an hour).

Peregrine-watchers have a lot in common with anglers who sit for hours, waiting for the bite that never comes. But at moments like this it is as much as I can do to leave the cliffs and head for home.

❦

OUT in the heavy clay country of the Marshwood Vale, the mighty field oaks stand tall; each one a living memorial to the days when the very survival of the nation depended on these magnificent old giants. Which is why, if ever there was one tree to cherish above all, then surely it is the English oak, whose strength and longevity has been admired down the centuries.

Oak was once England's natural canopy. Even when Henry VIII came to the throne a third of the country was still under its shade. But demands for its durable timber soon took their toll. Only the oak and its crooked branches could provide shipwrights with curved frames

ENGLISH OAK *Quercus robur*

and brackets strong enough to hold a 74-gun warship together as she lumbered up the Channel in a force eight gale.

By Nelson's time, good English oak was hard to come by, as enormous logs were needed for the stern posts and deck beams of a ship of the line, and the construction of a single vessel could swallow up 2,000 trees.

Of those that remain, wherever they grow, each one is a living nature reserve. From the caterpillars of the purple hairstreak butterflies which browse on its crown to the badgers that burrow at its roots, the oak is a high-rise tenement, host to hundreds of plants, insects, birds and animals.

Centuries of leaf-fall produce a rich loam in which bluebells, primroses and wood anemones thrive. Jays compete for its acorns with wood mice. The mice themselves become food for the tawny owls which nest in its hollow trunks as the tree grows older and, even at the end of its 250-year reign, its importance in the web of life continues as woodpeckers drill holes in its stag-headed branches.

'OWNING a moth trap,' said my friend Simon Barnes, the distinguished nature writer, 'is like taking part in a lucky dip – and every day is different.' He is right, too. When I open it up in the mornings, I never know what I will find, and June always promises an abundance of surprises.

Although there are moths on the wing every month of the year it is in June that they really come into their own. Well over 2,500 species have been recorded in the British Isles, including migrants that have flown in from as far away as Africa. Yet compared with butterflies – a miserly total of barely 67 species – moths have always taken second place in popularity.

Yet species such as the tiger moths are every bit as colourful as butterflies, as are the wonderful old-fashioned names bequeathed to them by our Victorian ancestors: the maiden's blush, the satin lutestring, the Clifden nonpareil. But their largely nocturnal lifestyles have condemned them to be the beauties born to blush unseen.

My latest haul has yielded at least a dozen species. Among them are buff-tips, white ermines, yellow underwings, a striped wainscot and a burnished brass; but most spectacular are the hawkmoths – large, strong-flying insects capable of speeds of up to 15 miles an hour (24 kilometres an hour). Only nine are resident species of which I have been lucky enough to trap four: privet hawkmoth, poplar hawkmoth, eyed hawkmoth and elephant hawkmoth.

Of these, the elephant hawkmoth – named after its larvae whose front ends extend like an elephant's trunk – is by far the most striking. Its colours are an unusual combination of olive green and pink, and at rest its wings fold back in the shape of an arrowhead. It is a creature of exquisite beauty.

Most hawkmoths feed after dark – hence the species lured into my trap. The one outstanding exception is the hummingbird hawkmoth, a Mediterranean immigrant that looks like its namesake. It arrives this month and you may see it later in the year, darting and hovering around nectar-rich garden plants such as buddleia and valerian while unfolding its watch-spring proboscis to feed.

When flying, its wings are a blur, moving at the incredible rate of 50 beats a second, which creates an audible humming noise. And, unlike other moths and butterflies, it has developed the ability to side-slip in mid-flight – probably to avoid being snapped up by predators.

Growing up in the London suburbs, I became fascinated by the caterpillars of the larger species such as the privet hawkmoth with their fat green bodies as big as my fingers. To track them down I would search for the frass (droppings) deposited on the pavements beneath the front garden lilacs or privet hedges on which they browsed. Then I'd keep them in jam jars, feeding them daily until they pupated.

Now, decades on and happily relocated in Dorset, it is the adult insects that I catch and release. Eagerly, I lift the lid to see which species have been lured inside by the trap's unearthly pale glow. Seldom do I find a rarity, but each one is a priceless living work of art.

IF you are in favour of badger culling, look away now. An article in *BBC Wildlife* magazine pulled no punches when describing the government's attempts to prevent the spread of bovine TB as a national disgrace. Its author, Mark Carwardine, is a zoologist and highly respected writer renowned for his outspoken views on conservation.

My own views are hopelessly ambivalent. As a child growing up during the war I was evacuated to Cornwall where I lived on a farm and learnt to milk the cows by hand, leaning my forehead on their warm flanks as the pail frothed between my knees. I cannot imagine the thought of having to put them down, quite apart from the crippling costs involved.

No wonder the farming community has been so supportive of the cull. If indeed it is the answer, who in all conscience could object? But as Mark Carwardine's exposé shows, there is no conclusive evidence to prove the badger is public enemy number one in transmitting bovine TB to cattle. While culling appears to be working in some areas, the government's own figures show that, overall, the problem is nowhere near being solved.

The slaughter began in 1975, resulting in the largest massacre of a protected species in living memory, and instead of solving the problem it has looked suspiciously as if the government has simply been sidestepping the issue to save face.

The answer, so Mark Carwardine has always believed, is the development of a cattle vaccine. 'The UK's cattle are already vaccinated for as many as 16 diseases,' he says, 'so why should TB be any different?'

THERE is nothing like a spell of lockdown to turn the spotlight on the wildlife to be found in the garden. Of late, instead of scooting off to Powerstock Common or watching peregrines at Thorncombe Beacon, I have been compelled to stay at home and get to know the resident fauna.

They have included a beautiful grass snake, nearly four feet (just over a metre) long and easily identified by its yellow collar, which slithered off when I disturbed it and swam across the stream at the bottom of the orchard; but equally fascinating to observe have been the newts which have silently colonised our garden pond.

Where did they come from, these beady-eyed jam-jar dinosaurs? Being amphibians, they are perfectly happy to live on land, hiding through the day to emerge to feed at night and hibernating under stones in winter; but how they got here is a mystery.

GRASS SNAKE *Natrix natrix*

We are blessed with two species: the palmate newt, which is the smallest of our three native species, and the common or smooth newt, the most numerous. Sadly, the great crested newt with its bright orange belly has not yet made an appearance, although we live in hope.

Earlier in the year the pond was seething with tadpoles, but newts are carnivorous and have been demonstrating the law of nature, red in tooth and claw to deadly effect. With luck, some may survive, together with other denizens such as the dragonfly nymphs with their bulbous eyes and fearsome pincers, soon to emerge as adult insects, darting and glittering in the summer sun.

JULY

HIGH summer, and the air over Dorset is sultry, unstirred. Cloud castles are building in the midday haze and the horseflies are biting. In short, haymaking weather.

Making hay is essentially a midsummer affair. Traditionally it was cut on St John's Day (24th June), but here in the southwest the custom has always been to wait until July, allowing the 'bottom grasses' to thicken up.

Sadly, old meadowland – the living tapestry that covered so much of England – has been casually discarded with scarcely a thought. Since 1949 Dorset has lost more than 95 per cent of its unimproved lowland meadows, which is par for the course over the whole country. While we have been busy protecting our most iconic wildlife species – otters, peregrines and ospreys – someone has stolen the grass from beneath our feet. But at least a few precious fragments survive, and the best belong to Kingcombe.

Here in the back of beyond beside the little River Hooke is a 19th-century landscape of unshorn hedgerows and pristine hay meadows filled with a litany of wild flowers. Back in the early 1980s, the land belonged to Arthur Walbridge, who continued to farm like his forefathers had done.

While those around him were busily acquiring the machines and chemicals of modern-day agriculture, he continued to make his hay without recourse to herbicides and artificial fertilisers. When he died in 1985, the Dorset Wildlife Trust stepped in and bought the farm, since when it has become one of their flagship properties.

Kingcombe's hay meadows belong to a way of life that allowed nature and humankind to co-exist. Here, fertilised by nothing more scientific than a good old-fashioned cowpat, the ancient sward still flourishes, comprised of scores of flowering plants and a dozen different grasses, including the sweet vernal grass whose plumed panicles release the essence of summer when cut, thanks to a natural oil called coumarin that gives old meadows their new-mown fragrance.

No wonder the Nature Conservancy rushed to designate it as a Site of Scientific Interest, and 'The Farm that Time Forgot' was eventually combined with neighbouring Powerstock Common in June 2021 to become England's newest National Nature Reserve.

Today, its 600 acres (2.5 square kilometres) are managed as a traditional working farm, complete with cows and sheep, its pastures enriched by nothing more radical than a cowpat, and the result is there for all to see.

In the 19th century the naturalist Richard Jefferies could still write about the corncrakes that skulked in the hay meadows of southern England. Their rasping cries, like running a finger down the teeth of a comb, were as familiar as the cuckoo. Now the corncrake has been banished to the outermost Scottish islands and even at Kingcombe the cuckoo's voice is seldom heard.

Yet the farm and its old-fashioned fields have survived to remind us of the countryside we once took for granted, where every summer the grass stands tall, thigh deep if you were to wade through it, stirring up butterflies at every step. In July, swallows swoop over the toppling grass heads. Marbled white butterflies sun themselves on knapweed flowers. Bumblebees drone among the meadow thistles and grasshoppers give the heat a voice, drowsy and quivering like the air itself.

The parish map of 1868 lists all the fields: Yonder Cowleaze, Mowlands Common, Lord's Mead. Today their names are all but forgotten, like those of the labourers who swung the scythes and forked the hay and unknowingly left us a corner of heaven to enjoy on a summer's day.

JULY is a good time to shine a spotlight on a truly special insect. Meet the glow-worm – which is not a worm at all, but a beetle. When I was a boy, they were so common in some localities that people could even read by their light.

Nowadays, sadly, they are a rare sight; but luckily for us, southern England is the best place to find them, and Dorset is as good as anywhere. Badbury Rings, Portland Bill and Corfe Castle are all glow-worm hotspots. Nearer to home, they have also been recorded on Eggardon Hill and Powerstock Common, and last month we were lucky enough to find two of them here, alive and glowing at night in our garden.

Glow-worms take their name from the female, who emits the light to attract a mate. The light itself is created by a substance called luciferin, which is found in the last three segments of her underside. Its greenish glow is surprisingly intense for such a small insect, and the keen-eyed males can pick her out from 30 feet (9 metres) away.

JERSEY TIGER MOTH *Euplagia quadripunctaria*

Unlike the wingless female, the males can fly, and have a pair of wing cases, making them look like true beetles. After mating, the eggs are laid in vegetation close to the ground, and when they hatch, the larvae feed primarily on small snails. It may come as a surprise to discover that the larvae themselves can also give out the faintest glow, and even the eggs can emit light; but nothing to compare with the ethereal emerald glimmer of the amorous adult female.

Now is also the time to start looking out for the Jersey tiger moth, a nationally scarce resident and summer migrant that is on the wing from mid-July onwards. With its chocolate-and-white zebra-striped forewings and blood orange hindwings this gorgeous day-flying moth is hard to miss, especially when sipping nectar on a sweet-scented buddleia bush. Once largely confined to the Channel Islands it has now gained a firm foothold on Dorset's Jurassic Coast and is steadily extending its range inland. In West Milton, I have recorded them every summer for the past three years, together with the garden tiger, whose 'woolly bear' caterpillars I once collected as a child.

AUGUST

AMAZING, the things you see when you look up at the heavens. One day recently, confined to my garden recliner as a result of a bad back, I lay stretched out in the sun with nothing to do and my eyes fixed firmly skyward. It was one of those all-too-rare days with only a few cumulus clouds to interrupt the faultless blue vaults above.

It was also a perfect flying day. That much was obvious from the way a flock of gulls was riding the thermals, spiralling effortlessly upwards until they were lost to view.

Revelling in the midsummer warmth, I slipped into a kind of reverie, broken from time to time by the flickering shapes of swallows and house martins swooping overhead as if enjoying the sheer thrill of flying.

Further off, rooks rose and fell across the valley over Milton Mill, and a raven announced its presence with a guttural croak as it rowed through the air on the lookout for carrion.

RED KITE *Milvus milvus*

Then, high above me, a large raptor with long wings and a forked tail sailed past, outlined in perfect silhouette against the blue. I knew straight away what it was: a red kite – even though it was the first I had seen in Dorset.

Although one of our biggest birds of prey with a wingspan of over five feet (one-and-a-half metres), red kites weigh less than a buzzard. The reason lies in their lifestyle, for these lords of the air are as light as thistledown, designed to soar for long periods, saving their energy to ride the thermals as they scour the land below for carrion.

My first glimpse of these elegant raptors took place in January 1985, when I had followed the course of the River Ystwyth into the lonely hills of Ceredigion in the company of Roger Lovegrove, the RSPB's Chief Officer for Wales. There, with the light fading and snow slanting down, we watched more than 30 spiralling into the woods to roost.

At that time, they represented one-quarter of all the red kites of Wales, for the species was still clawing its way back from near extinction in 1931, when only one breeding female was left in the whole of the UK.

Since then, they have continued their remarkable comeback, rescued from virtual extinction by one of the world's longest-running protection programmes. Today's population stands at around 1,800 breeding pairs and are a common sight in the Chilterns for anyone driving down the M40 from London to Oxford. Now, as their numbers continue to grow, it could be only a matter of time before they become a familiar addition to our own Dorset skies.

THE creation of our national parks has been one of the most outstanding environmental achievements of the past 100 years. We now have 15. The Peak District is the oldest, created in 1951. The newest is the South Downs, established in 2010, and moves are afoot to add Dorset to the list.

The idea of a national park for Dorset has been around since 1945; but while other parks have been up and running for decades, Dorset has remained on the drawing board.

Now the dream has been resurrected. The case for a Dorset and East Devon national park was submitted to Natural England in 2013 and has been favourably received, offering hope to all its supporters that it could become a reality in a few years' time.

With much-loved landscapes everywhere at risk the least we can do is try to protect the last of the best we have left. That is why the national park concept was devised in the first place, along with Areas of Outstanding Natural Beauty such as the Dorset AONB, the second biggest in England, covering most of the Jurassic Coast and including the area in which I live.

National parks provide a patchwork of stunning countryside protected by laws that ensure they will be conserved and enhanced, while recognising their importance as living landscapes, supporting rural communities such as ours. In addition, the benefits to Dorset's holiday industry would be enormous should it acquire national park status. Since the South Downs national park was set up it has benefited to the tune of an extra £100 million in tourist revenue, so upgrading the Dorset AONB looks like a classic no-brainer.

OF all the birds that light up our skies every summer, few give me more pleasure than the hobby. In flight this fierce little falcon resembles a giant swift as it swoops and flickers through the air in search of prey, which it catches and eats on the wing.

The hobby is also one of the few raptors agile enough to take swifts and swallows, although dragonflies are their favourite food – hence their presence around wetlands such as the Somerset Levels.

When perched they resemble a miniature peregrine, but there is no mistaking their rust-red 'trousers' – or the moustachial stripes on each side of the bill which give them the look of a Mexican bandit. Their Latin name, *Falco subbuteo*, translates as 'falcon smaller than a buzzard,' and gave rise to the popular table-football game because it was the designer's favourite bird!

Their winter home is sub-Saharan Africa, where I have watched them hunting over the Rufiji River in Tanzania's vast Selous Game Reserve; but in March they arrive in Britain to breed, usually appropriating an old crow's nest in which to lay their two or three eggs. By the end of summer, the chicks are fledged and ready to undertake the long journey back to Africa, making August one of the best times to see them.

Eggardon Hill has always been a happy hunting ground for watching the hobby in action. Twice I have been there in the last couple of months, and on both occasions, I have been treated to a breathtaking flypast by these dashing predators. Of course, there is no guarantee that you will see one. But their sudden appearance is always a possibility until they depart before the onset of autumn.

☙

LAST month it was moths under the spotlight. Now it is time for butterflies to take centre stage as our summer insect migrants arrive. And foremost among them is the painted lady, the world's most widely distributed species and the only one recorded in Iceland.

These fast-flying beauties reach our shores after a marathon journey from North Africa, and whenever I see them my mind rewinds to my suburban childhood. I grew up in the Blitz during World War II, when weeds and garden flowers ran riot amidst the rubble, transforming bomb sites into rampant jungles of raspberry canes and dense thickets of willowherb over which the cloying scent of buddleia bushes hung like a cheap perfume.

Those were the summers of the great invasion, not by Rommel's Panzers but by swarms of butterflies. In the local park, where trenches

PAINTED LADY *Vanessa cardui*

had been dug across the open fields to prevent Nazi warplanes landing, thousands of tortoiseshell butterflies sunned themselves on the tall thistles that had sprung unbidden from the earth.

As the summer advanced, clouds of migrant butterflies – peacocks, painted ladies, red admirals and clouded yellows – poured across the Channel to settle on the bomb-site buddleias where they clung in clusters, sucking up the nectar until they were almost too drunk to fly.

Today, the suburbia I knew – bomb sites, air-raid shelters, elm trees and all – has become part of a sepia world as remote to me as Tudor England; but our Dorset garden still attracts its share of painted ladies, and whenever I return to my suburban roots, now scarcely recognisable with its carports and loft conversions, my mind runs back to those butterfly years when the sun shone and the buddleia flowered and summer seemed as if it could never end.

IF ever there was a vote for Britain's most endearing mammal the hazel dormouse would win hands down. With its chubby little body and lustrous black eyes (essential for its nocturnal lifestyle) it is by far our most attractive small rodent, distinguished from all other mice by its thick, furry tail.

Sadly, dormice are no longer common, having declined as the practice of hazel coppicing fell out of favour, and are today a protected species. In summer they come out only at night to search for insects, nuts and flowers which they hold in their forepaws as they nibble, and from October until April they sleep all winter through, curled up in a nest of dry leaves and grasses often hidden in an old hazel stool. The young are born in August – four or five to a litter – and must weigh at least half an ounce (12 grams) before hibernating if they are to survive their first winter.

The fact that West Dorset is one of Britain's few dormouse strongholds should be a cause for local celebration, even if they are so rarely encountered that it must have come as a surprise when their presence was discovered at the site chosen for Powerstock's new affordable housing project.

Due to their protected status care must be taken to avoid undue disturbance. In December 2007, in what is believed to have been the first ever UK conviction involving dormice, Bridgend County Borough Council was fined £1,000 plus £100 costs after pleading guilty to an offence under the 1981 Wildlife and Countryside Act – the primary piece of legislation designed to protect the UK's wildlife.

Today, local authorities are far more rigorous in upholding the law and it has been good to see our own West Dorset District planners have been going to great lengths to ensure that Powerstock's residents – humans and dormice – should continue to co-exist.

HIGH summer, and a pair of buzzards circling overhead in the thermals. There is no mistaking their mewling cries or the distinctive shape of their broad, blunt wings, held in a shallow V as they turn on the wind, rising ever higher into the blue until they are mere specks, drifting over the hills towards Loders.

The two or three blotchy white eggs laid in a stick nest back in the spring will have hatched long ago, and in August the hungry youngsters are also on the wing. However, even when fully fledged they stay with their parents, who will continue to feed them for another eight weeks until they become truly independent.

Now begins the hardest time in their lives, when three-quarters of all young buzzards die, mostly due to starvation, before reaching maturity at the age of three years.

BUZZARD *Buteo buteo*

Yet despite such hardships the common buzzard is found over most of Europe and as far as Mongolia and Siberia. In Britain, which has a breeding population of well over 60,000 pairs, it is our commonest bird of prey and is well established in Dorset. You seldom need to drive too far along our local lanes to spot a buzzard sailing over the fields or perched on a telephone pole, eyes peeled for the rabbits, voles and carrion that form a major part of its diet; and in winter when foraging is harder for all wildlife, it is not unusual to find as many as a dozen buzzards picking over a ploughed field in search of earthworms.

Their round heads sometimes give them a slightly owlish appearance and their colour can vary, especially their brown and white wing patterns when seen from below; and it is always worth giving them the once-over in case they should turn out to be a honey buzzard or – rarer still – a rough-legged buzzard.

A buzzard aloft somehow lacks the élan of the sickle-winged hobby, the dash of the sparrowhawk or the breathtaking speed and power of the peregrine. Yet for me, more than any other raptor, its plaintive voice and slowly circling silhouette in the skies above Eggardon encapsulate the timeless appeal of the West Dorset countryside.

IT is going to be a hot day on the Chesil Beach. Already its tawny flanks are shimmering in the morning haze and the voice of the sea is hushed, like the gasp of a heavy sleeper as the ebb tide laps at the sloping shore.

Crunching over its empty tidelines on my way from West Bexington to Abbotsbury, I remind myself that I am walking on one of the geological wonders of Europe. This mighty ridge is deservedly protected as part of Dorset's Jurassic Coast World Heritage Site.

Curling around Lyme Bay for 18 miles (30 kilometres), its 180 billion pebbles have been graded by the prevailing tides, and what is known as the longshore drift. At West Bay they consist mostly of pea gravel, but the further east you travel the bigger they become until at Portland they are the size of skulls. That is why, it was said, smugglers landing here in the dead of night could judge where they were simply by looking at the size of the stones on the beach.

In winter there is no shelter from the wild south-westerlies that drove many a ship to its doom in the age of sail; and in summer the beach is a burning desert. Yet some plants still take root among the stones and even thrive under the sea wind: thrift and campion, prickly clumps of sea holly and yellow horned-poppies with long, curly seed pods like a witch's fingernails.

Birds also frequent the Chesil, which is home to a colony of little terns – the second-rarest breeding bird in Britain. But the birdwatcher's first port of call is always the Fleet, a magical wilderness of whispering reed beds whose brackish waters have been home to hundreds of mute swans since the reign of the Plantagenet kings.

Running from Abbotsbury to Portland, it is Britain's biggest tidal lagoon, and it is here that the Bank assumes its full stature, rising in a 40-foot-high (12-metre-high) ridge between the Fleet and the sea.

IN August, our garden echoes to the sounds of summer. Wood pigeons call with husky voices and from every lavender bed comes the dynamo hum of honeybees on their tireless search for nectar.

Back in June we had wondered if our bees would survive. For when Annabelle inspected her hive one morning, she discovered that no eggs were being laid, signifying the loss of the queen.

There was only one way to save our precious colony of 50,000 honeybees. A new ready-mated queen was purchased for £40, but while she was being placed in the hive the original queen was found. Somehow, she had managed to climb through the queen excluder into the supers – the upper chambers where the honey is stored – and was busily laying eggs.

Emergency measures were called for to avoid civil war in the hive. So, hurriedly, Annabelle removed the new queen together with her workers and placed her in a brood box where she has now started to produce a healthy second colony.

During these proceedings Annabelle found that one super was already full and ready for harvesting. The combs were placed in a centrifugal extractor and spun off, resulting in 20 pounds (9 kilograms)

HONEYBEE *Apis mellifera*

of honey whose distinctively strong flavour and deep amber colour reminded us of the delicious wild forest honey we have tasted on our travels in Zambia and East Africa.

In previous years our Spick Hatch honey has always been of the palest gold in colour, and with a delicate flavour, giving rise to the question: which flower species have our bees been visiting this year to produce that richer, darker honey?

Meanwhile, there is still time for them to continue gathering nectar. The end of the month is usually the time when beekeepers remove honey from the hive; and given good weather it is even possible to wait a few weeks longer. So long may the sun continue to shine, and the bees bless us with their drowsy serenade – not to mention their sweet end-of-summer bounty.

SEPTEMBER

BROWSING through my latest copy of the *Dorset Wildlife Trust Magazine* I was horrified to discover how many of the familiar words that shaped my childhood are dying out. Apparently, the *Oxford Junior Dictionary* has consigned a host of nature-related words to the scrapheap and replaced them with new words and phrases such as blog and chatroom.

The following are among the words to have been dropped:

Acorn; adder; ash; beech; blackberry; bluebell; bramble; brook; buttercup; catkin; clover; conker; cowslip; cygnet; dandelion; fern; fungus; gorse; hazel; hazelnut; heather; heron; holly; horse chestnut; ivy; kingfisher; lark; magpie; minnow; newt; otter; pansy; pasture; poppy; porpoise; primrose; raven; starling; stoat; stork; sycamore; thrush; weasel; violet; willow; wren.

Having typed out this list I realise I have unintentionally written a valedictory poem for our vanishing countryside. For me, every one of these words conjures up the spirit of never-to-be-forgotten places where I came face to face with the natural world and its treasures for the first time. The colour of bluebells; the taste of blackberries crushed on the tongue; the coconut scent of golden gorse; and the grunt of a raven tumbling in free fall over Cornwall's Atlantic clifftops.

How desperately sad, that a whole generation is growing up who has never seen a starling, caught a minnow, climbed an ash tree or read *Tarka the Otter*. No wonder this cull by the OJD in favour of words from the digital world has been met with outrage by conservationists and authors alike.

Should we be worried? I believe we should. It is just another step on the slippery slope whereby humanity is becoming increasingly separated from the living world. And the gulf is widening year on year. A report by Natural England discovered that less than 10 per cent of children play in wild areas compared with 40 per cent of adults when they were young; and a recent YouGov study with the Wildlife Trusts found that 78 per cent of parents are concerned that their children don't spend enough time with nature and wildlife.

❧

DOWN in the orchard sits a butterfly, ragged wings pressed close together. When they are open it is a joy to behold, all glowing gold and butterscotch brown; but at rest it looks more like a dead oak leaf – a perfect camouflage designed to protect it from hungry birds.

It is a comma, its name derived from the single white punctuation mark on the underside of each hindwing, and it has been feeding, greedily sucking up the sweet juices of our windfall apples – the last of the summer wine.

COMMA *Polygonia c-album*

Butterflies were one of the favourite subjects of my friend Gordon Beningfield, the wildlife artist whose paintings of rural life had made him hugely popular. Gordon lived in Hertfordshire, but clearly Dorset's insect-friendly countryside had stolen his heart away, and in the days when I lived in Powerstock he was a regular visitor. That is why, whenever I see a comma I think of Gordon, whose exquisite watercolour sketches capture its understated beauty to perfection.

Together with red admirals and other species, commas are still regular visitors to our garden, but never in the numbers I remember as a boy. Nowadays, butterflies and all insects are fewer everywhere – hence the call to arms issued by the Wildlife Trusts in which they implore the government to reverse this catastrophic decline.

Their basic message is that we need insects, and unless we act now, future generations will not be able to enjoy the butterflies, moths, ladybirds, dragonflies, ground beetles and bumblebees that grace our countryside. Furthermore, say the Wildlife Trusts, the ability to feed ourselves will be compromised and many of our beloved birds, mammals and other species will simply disappear.

SOMETHING nasty in the woodshed? Not a bit of it. For the past two years we have been sharing our lives with one of Britain's most elusive inhabitants. It is the lesser horseshoe bat, a mammal included in the Red List, an inventory of the world's most threatened species compiled by the International Union for Conservation of Nature.

Just imagine: a tiny creature sharing the same conservation status as the panda, hanging out in the roof space above our winter log pile. Last year there were five. Now there are 12, so they must be happy with their surroundings. During the day they are just discernible in the gloom, dangling from the rafters like ripe, furry plums. But at dusk they emerge to hunt over the garden, snapping up moths and other insects.

Just how rare are they? According to the Dorset Bat Group only three known nursery sites remain in this county, with a population unlikely to exceed 300 individual animals. But it is good to know that Dorset is something of a bat stronghold, with no less than 14 different species, ranging in size from the noctule bat with its 16-inch (40-centimetre) wingspan to the tiny pipistrelle or flittermouse.

One of the best ways to identify the different species is to buy a bat detector – a handheld device that can pick up the high-frequency sounds emitted by bats in flight.

These echolocation sounds act as a kind of radar, enabling bats to find their way around in the dark, but are beyond the range of human hearing. However, a bat detector can pick them up as a series of audible clicks whose different frequencies enable the user to identify one species from another.

In September, with autumn approaching, all bat species will be busily feeding and fattening up before hibernating, and our resident lesser horseshoes will soon forsake their summer roost in our woodshed to crawl away into cracks and crevices to sleep the winter through.

IT'S a steep climb to the top of Golden Cap, the highest cliff on the Channel coast, but at 627 feet (191 metres) above the sea, the views from the summit are reward enough. To the west, beyond Charmouth and Lyme Regis, you can follow the curve of Lyme Bay past East Devon's share of the Jurassic Coast as far as Start Point. Eastward, it is the corrugated sandstone wall of West Bay's cliffs that catches the eye, and the Chesil Beach beyond.

Then turn your back on the sea to find the Marshwood Vale laid out at your feet, a sleepy hollow of wet meadows, old hazel coppices and great field oaks, encircled by no less than seven prehistoric hill forts.

A glance at the Ordnance Survey map reveals a green web of public footpaths and bridleways, but their presence hides a guilty secret. Should you wish to go exploring off the beaten track, it may come as a shock to learn that only 8 per cent of Britain's countryside is accessible to the public; and although England and Wales have 144,000 miles (232,000 kilometres) of public footpaths, they account for only 0.3 per cent of the land mass. Hardly surprising when half of England is still owned by just 1 per cent of the population – an uncomfortable reminder that we are still living in a leftover feudal landscape.

Ninety years have passed since 500 mill- and steelworkers from Manchester and Sheffield set off on their mass trespass at Kinder Scout in the Derbyshire Peak District. It was their determination that kick-started the creation of the UK's national parks; and yet unlike in Scotland, France and Scandinavia, the right to roam remains a dream.

Nor is it likely to happen any time soon. The trouble is that with the right comes responsibility, and landowners know to their cost what happens when visitors (unfamiliar with country ways) leave behind them a long trail of litter, farm gates left open and livestock savaged or killed by dogs.

JAY *Garrulus glandarius*

WITH its black moustache and a raucous voice like tearing linen, the jay is not difficult to identify. But don't be fooled by its cinnamon plumage and gaudy blue wing bars. It is still a corvid – a member of the crow family – possessing all the dark arts of its bigger relatives. Robbing other birds' nests of their eggs and young have earnt it a bad reputation that overshadows its true value as the unsung creator of England's oak woods.

That is because acorns are the jay's staple diet in winter. Plucked ripe from the tree, the oak tree's fruit is hungrily gobbled up, and what they can't eat now will be buried in the ground beneath the forest carpet of moss and leaves. It is estimated that one bird can carry up to nine acorns in its gullet and may bury as many as 5,000 in a single autumn of which some are sure to germinate.

Jays possess an extraordinary ability to remember where their caches are hidden – even under a winter snowfall. Yet inevitably, not all are recovered, and those left behind eventually take root to emerge as oak saplings in the spring. In this way our oak woods have been naturally replenished and maintained over the years.

So, next time you see a jay, don't curse it for being a nest robber. Without its fondness for acorns, the great oaks whose timbers gave birth to Nelson's warships might never have flourished had it not been for the industrious jay and its occasional memory lapses.

❧

AM I alone in watching with dismay as Himalayan balsam spreads like a rash across the face of West Dorset? Ever since June its clusters of sickly-sweet flowers have been blooming along our lanes and riverbanks. Now the flowering time is over. The seeds are set – up to 800 for every plant – and ripe for uncontrolled dispersal. All it takes is the slightest movement and the pods explode like grapeshot, travelling up to 22 feet (7 metres) away to lay down the next generation of these unwelcome alien invaders.

Introduced to Britain in 1839, this head-high relative of the busy Lizzie took only ten years to jump over the garden wall to freedom, since when it has spread to all parts of Britain. In Liverpool it is known as Mersey weed. Elsewhere it goes by other names: gnome's hatstand (because of its helmet-shaped flowers) and kiss-me-on-the-mountain. But do not be taken in by its flamboyant displays of orchid-pink blossoms. Himalayan balsam is one of the thugs of the plant world, ruthlessly elbowing our native plants aside.

Today, so entrenched is this insidious menace that concerned bodies such as the National Trust reckon it could cost up to £300 million to wipe it from the face of Britain.

Using weedkillers to eradicate it from its favourite riverbank habitat is difficult because of the risk of contaminating our waterways; but there is a chink in its armour. Simply grab the plant by its fleshy rhubarb-coloured stem and give it a tug. It is so shallow-rooted that it just gives up the ghost – so much easier than pulling ragwort.

We started doing this on our own modest section of the Mangerton Brook – sometimes taking to the water in thigh-boot waders to reach the most inaccessible plants. Now, after two summers of rigorous weed pulling, we are seeing the benefit, although we still have not managed to eradicate it completely.

❧

THERE'S a bunch of feathered assassins on the loose in West Milton. They spend their days asleep, holed up among the ivy-covered trees on the surrounding hillsides, but as soon as it is dark, they emerge from their hideouts to rend the air with their quavering calls, striking terror into the hearts of the local rodent population.

Tawny owls are our most widespread birds of prey and September is a good time to hear them. This is when the youngsters disperse from their natal areas to seek territories of their own, and when the adults are also noisily reclaiming their home patches.

The best time to hear them is when they are hunting, from around 9pm onwards until dawn, and there is no mistaking the male's long-drawn-out *hu-hoo-ooo*, or the female's eerily familiar *kewick, kewick*.

TAWNY OWL *Strix aluco*

As a child, growing up in suburban Surrey, their other-worldly cries used to make the hair stand up on the back of my neck as I lay in bed in the small hours, but in time I grew to love them, recognising them as voices from the retreating countryside that no amount of development had been able to banish entirely.

Now I listen out for them with increased enjoyment, revelling in such moments as when sometimes they perch in the walnut tree outside our bedroom window, or call to each other from the roof.

A few years ago, to impress my grandchildren, I tried to attract a male tawny owl, imitating its call by blowing through my cupped hands. Every time I called it answered, drawing closer every time until at last it came silently swooping into the beech tree above our heads.

There it sat, its plumage the colour of the old year's leaves, glaring down at us with its huge round eyes. I am not sure who was the more surprised – myself or the children. But when I tried the same trick the following night it was a complete failure. Clearly, tawny owls are more intelligent than I thought.

TAWNY owls are not the only nocturnal visitors to take up residence in our valley. For over a month now I have been delighting in the ghostly presence of a pair of barn owls. When I first came to Dorset back in the late 1960s, I used to watch these mysterious birds on late summer evenings, drifting over the meadows in the last of the light; but not since I moved to West Milton had I seen them regularly again until now.

Although barn owls are nocturnal by nature, they often emerge an hour or two before sunset, and for this reason I always think of them as spirits of the twilight zone, soundlessly floating through the dusk in search of mice and voles.

With their lightweight bodies and long, rounded wings they are masters of the air, able to fly at low speeds, jinking and hovering before pouncing on some unsuspecting rodent. They are also blessed with good night vision and ears so sharp it is said they can tell the difference between a scampering vole and the sound of the wind in the grass.

As for the noises that barn owls make, they hiss, twitter, click and snore, but never hoot. Unlike the familiar calls of tawny owls, the barn owl emits a wheezing shriek – hence its other name: the screech owl.

In recent decades, farm chemicals, rat poison, traffic and wet weather have all contributed to the barn owl's decline. The intensification of agriculture has swept away much of the old meadowland and rough pasture which harboured its prey, creating a vicious spiral in which fewer voles mean fewer owls, and most pairs can raise only one brood each year instead of two. Yet Britain still has a breeding population of around 4,000 pairs.

A resident pair will typically hunt across a home range of about one square mile (three square kilometres), hiding by day among the rafters of a suitable farm building. For weeks I wondered where our pair were roosting, until one evening I looked inside a remote hillside barn and found the telltale pellets of compacted fur and mouse bones they had disgorged after their midnight feasts.

OCTOBER

DUSK comes early in October. Frost in the hedges, lights coming on, the village enclosed in a bell jar of stillness. And in the garden, a robin singing. For me, when other songbirds have fallen silent or flown south to Africa, that sad little evensong is a comforting sound, reaffirming that at least one resident is prepared to stay put and see the winter through. But to another robin those silvery cadences carry an unmistakeable warning. Keep out! For if truth be told this bright-eyed songster is a bit of a thug.

That is because territory is what makes Cock Robin tick. He spends most of his life acquiring it, and most of his energy in singing and fighting over it. A robin's home patch may be as little as half an acre (2,000 square metres), but its boundaries are well-defined, and woe betide the rival that oversteps the line.

So how did such a bossy little bird become a traditional feature of our Christmas scene? The answer is provided by the Post Office.

Expansion of the postal system in Queen Victoria's reign gave rise to what was then the novel fashion of sending Christmas greeting cards – delivered by postmen who wore bright red uniforms and thus became affectionately known as 'robins'.

Once more from the gloom falls the same sweet soliloquy. A sudden flutter of wings and he lights on the handle of my garden fork, almost close enough to touch. Pugnacious little backyard bruiser he may be. But how empty my autumn garden would be without his jaunty, head-on-one-side figure, his beady eye and red badge of courage.

THE way into the wood is as dark as a cave. Once inside, I follow a path across boggy ground between shaggy clumps of pendulous sedge and stunted oaks with mossy limbs. Welcome to Powerstock Common.

No ordinary nature reserve, this. It is a precious relic of the ancient woodlands that once covered much of Britain. Charcoal burners felled its finest trees a century or more ago. The Forestry Commission tried to smother it with conifers until they had a change of heart, but it has survived to this day, one of those diminishing scraps of land that remains defiantly wild.

In spring its derelict hazel coppices are awash with the scent of bluebells; but in October when the leaves begin to fall it bears witness to a dramatic rite of passage that marks the turning year.

The tracks in the mud are a dead giveaway. Those twin-toed slots are signs of the fallow deer that have haunted these woods since the Romans marched over the downs to Eggardon.

The bucks spend the summer as solitary wanderers, sometimes coalescing in small bachelor groups. But in October when the first frosts bite and the last trace of itching velvet has gone from their antlers, their behaviour undergoes a dramatic change. This is the time

FALLOW DEER *Dama dama*

of the rut, in which the veteran bucks are pumped up with testosterone and fight each other for the right to mate.

There is no mistaking their stamping grounds. In a muddy glade I came across just such a spot last year, a black wallow where a buck had rolled and trampled to mark his territory, rending the air with groans of love. But the lord of the ring was not at home and the wood was locked in a single silence.

I moved on, found a fallen tree, and sat down to wait as the light faded and the first stars appeared. Then it began, a rhythmic, rasping grunt, like a motorbike being kick-started. It was a fallow buck caught up in the throes of the rut, a sound as old as England itself. Once more he threw down his challenge, and this time he was answered as his rivals closed in and there followed a furious click-clack of antlers as the future of Powerstock's fallow herd was decided.

No chance of a sighting. They were hidden away in the deepest part of the wood, surrounded by an impenetrable tangle of chest-high brambles and blackthorn thickets and I had no wish to disturb them. But even as I rose to my feet, the fighting ended and a shadowy shape flitted through the trees, antlers laid back over its shoulders. The vanquished buck and I were taking our leave together.

THE grey squirrels are back in the walnut tree and no wonder. This year has produced a record crop and for once we were able to harvest a decent bagful of nuts before our uninvited guests helped themselves.

Walnuts are among the oldest foods known to humankind, dating back 8,000 years, and are found throughout much of the world from China to Mexico. Our English walnut trees originated in ancient Persia and were probably brought to this country via the Silk Route. Here they thrive well in our temperate climate, even though they are on the edge of their European range, which is why perhaps they put out their leaves so late in the year.

I always think the nuts taste best right now, eaten when freshly fallen from their split green husks. As for the tree itself, I love its silver-grey crocodile-skin bark and canopy of pinnate leaves. They remind me of the leadwood (*Combretum imberbe*), a distinctive feature of Botswana's Okavango Delta woodlands. But in Dorset, instead of hornbills and sleeping leopards, we have squirrels and a host of garden birds.

Nuthatches pipe from its crooked branches. Treecreepers scuttle up its fissured bole, winkling out spiders with their thin, curved bills.

COMMON WALNUT *Juglans regia*

In springtime great spotted woodpeckers drum on its hollow superstructure and wood pigeons hide in its summertime canopy, calling 'Don't cry so, Suzy' over and over through the golden days.

Now it is autumn and the weary old tree is pensioning off its leaves as the first frosts bite. Together with those of the beeches by the stream below, the hedgerow hazels and field maples, they create a last hurrah of glorious colour before the onset of winter. Time for us, too, to hasten indoors as the nights draw down, to light the fire in the inglenook and warm ourselves in the comforting glow of logs split and stacked the previous year.

❦

FIRST it was hedgehogs appearing all over West Milton. Now it is the turn of the not-so-lonesome polecat, a large chocolate-coloured member of the weasel family. Last week, West Milton resident and wildlife enthusiast Ian Mortimer captured one going about its nocturnal business in the village. Two days later he recorded a second sighting – but this time to his surprise it was a different animal.

Previously, I had seen a dead polecat in the lane to Loscombe, and a live one crossing the road one night in Melplash back in the winter. According to Ian, that makes the A3066 – the winding highway between Melplash and Beaminster – a polecat hotspot with reports of at least a dozen roadkills over the past couple of years.

All of which leads me to believe the species is now firmly established in Dorset. But it was not always thus. A century ago, polecats were on the verge of extinction after centuries of trapping and persecution due to their fondness for young pheasants and poultry. Hence their name, derived from the French word *poule*. They were also once known as foulmarts because of the glands at the base of the tail that give off a persistent and evil-smelling scent.

Only in wildest Wales did the polecat survive, since when it has been slowly but steadily extending its range, sometimes mating with escaped ferrets to produce hybrids with creamier pelage.

The return of this hedgerow bandit with its long, lithe body and highwayman's mask may be of concern to anyone who keeps chickens. But before you reach for your shotgun, remember that the polecat is also the farmer's friend with a taste for rabbits and small rodents, including rats.

WHAT a mysterious creature is the eel. Although the Mangerton is not a species-rich river it can still boast some interesting residents, including brown trout, sea trout, bullheads – and eels.

Recent excavations to improve the flow of the Milton Mill leat unearthed a fine specimen which hurriedly wriggled away to avoid the digger's metal teeth. It was the first eel I had seen for years and would tend to confirm that our modest little river is still in good heart.

EEL *Anguilla anguilla*

Eels have been with us for a very long time, and in the wetlands of East Anglia they grow to a prodigious size. One specimen weighing more than 20 pounds (9 kilograms) was caught near Norwich in 1839, and Ely is believed to have been named for the rent of 100,000 eels paid each year to the lord of the manor.

The eel I saw was in the fourth and final stage of its metamorphosis. Born as a tiny leaf-shaped larva somewhere off the coast of Cuba, it first becomes a translucent 'glass eel', finding its way to Europe on one of nature's most stupendous migrations. Here it morphs into an elver and finally an adult, sometimes remaining at sea for decades until some unknown impulse compels it to return from whence it came, during which time it will acquire a gender, digest its own innards and spawn before dying in the Sargasso Sea where its life began.

Sadly, eels are everywhere swimming towards extinction. Disease, pollution, pesticides and hydro-electric turbines all take their toll, as does fishing for glass eels in Spain and France. This custom also persisted in the Somerset Levels, and at this point I must confess to my own small contribution to their demise. There, a few years ago, I was once served a breakfast of glass eels fried in oil and garlic, and I am ashamed to admit they were delicious.

CAUGHT red-handed in the middle of the lawn, the intruder never stayed to argue the toss. With a contemptuous flick of its bushy tail, the grey squirrel was over the garden wall in a flash and heading for the trees.

Many of our most familiar mammals are incomers. It was the Normans who brought the fallow deer to Britain in the 11th century, followed later by the rabbit. But no other alien species has caused so much controversy as the grey squirrel.

Its true home is the oak and hickory woodlands of the eastern USA, from which it was first introduced in 1876 when a pair of greys were set loose in Henbury Park, near Macclesfield. Others followed, driving out our native red squirrels in the process, until today there are something like 2.7 million of these fleet-footed invaders in the UK.

Whether scampering through the treetops or foraging for fallen acorns in the grass of city parks, there is no denying their cute appeal. So how come the upstart greys have generated so much opprobrium?

According to the European Squirrel Initiative (ESI), the damage grey squirrels inflict on our broadleaved trees costs the UK economy an eye-watering £40 million a year, to say nothing of the threat they pose to nesting birds. No wonder they have become known as 'tree rats' whose unwelcome presence has resulted in the UK government stumping up £244,000 to develop an oral contraceptive which, it is hoped, will curb their impact and may even enable Dorset's red squirrels to expand from their last stronghold on Brownsea Island in Poole Harbour.

IN West Dorset we are blessed by living alongside one of the largest protected marine areas in the UK, a biodiversity hotspot in which vast areas of Lyme Bay have been closed to dredging and trawling.

The results have been spectacular. Last summer a local fisherman managed to film a giant humpback whale breaching close to his boat off Lyme Regis, and a small population of white-beaked dolphins have also taken up permanent residence in the Bay to the delight of all those lucky enough to watch them.

I was reminded of this during a recent trip down to the coast. The sun was shining. The Bay was calm, and every now and then, less than half a mile offshore, the sea would boil as shoals of mackerel chased

WHITE-BEAKED DOLPHIN *Lagenorhynchus albirostris*

their prey to the surface. They were feeding on whitebait, and to watch them 'straying', as the old-time fisherman would say, was a welcome sign that our local waters are in good shape.

The arrival of the sprats and the mackerel that feed on them happens every summer and continues long into the autumn. Sometimes they gather in such numbers that masses are washed ashore, creating a silvery tideline along the Chesil Beach as evidence of their desperate attempts to avoid being eaten.

But more than anything, it is the abundance of the mackerel that accounts for the presence of the white-beaked dolphins. Growing up to ten feet (three metres) in length and weighing as much as 770 pounds (350 kilograms), these elegant cetaceans are powerful swimmers, capable of speeds of up to 28 miles an hour (45 kilometres an hour).

Together with common, bottlenose and Risso's dolphins, they are one of no less than 28 cetacean species recorded in British waters, and among the seven species that occur regularly throughout the year.

To identify them from other species such as common and bottlenose dolphins, look for a large black animal with a distinctive white flash on its sides – and that unique white beak.

THE swallows have gone. The long nights are with us again, and the first frosts are due. Time to take stock and look back at one of the hottest summers for years. How quickly our parched fields and hillsides recovered after a few inches of rain; but we have yet to weigh up the cost, not only to our precious farmlands but also to our wildlife in terms of trees stressed out by drought and the knock-on effects felt by our most vulnerable butterfly species.

That is why it is worth thinking about 'Earth Overshoot Day' – the day when we have used up all the resources our planet can provide for the year. Alarmingly, we reached it back in August – the earliest Overshoot Day since we first began overusing the planet's natural resources in the 1970s.

According to the Global Footprint Network, the planet can no longer cope with our expanding appetite for its natural resources. Quite simply, there is no longer enough fish, fresh water and fertile soil to go round. And we British are among the worst culprits, using up so much that it would take a planet three times the size of ours to sustain itself if everyone was as profligate.

I came across this snippet of news in a copy of the *Daily Telegraph*. It was tucked away on the inside back page, along with the crossword and other trivia when it should have been splashed across the front page in giant headlines.

Following a summer of catastrophic wildfires in which half the world seemed to be going up in smoke, perhaps we should spare a thought as to how we will continue to feed ourselves if global warming continues to place our planet under ever-greater stress.

After all, such is the precarious nature of our high-tech 21st-century lifestyle that all it would take is one major hiccup between farm and plate, and most of us would be left just three meals away from disaster.

NOVEMBER

LEWESDON (915 feet/279 metres) and Pilsdon Pen (909 feet/ 277 metres) are Dorset's highest hills. Compared with the Scottish Highlands they are mere pimples, but they still provide a touch of grandeur when glimpsed across the Marshwood Vale.

Viewed from the sea, these twin eminences have been familiar daymarks to generations of local fishermen. The Cow and the Calf is what the old West Bay boatmen called them, although the difference in height between them is barely discernible. Both were once great Iron Age hill forts; but while Pilsdon stands bare against the sky, Lewesdon wears a crown of beech woods.

Unlike Surrey, where I was born, Dorset is not a woodland county, and I miss the pleasure of long walks in the lofty woodlands of the North Downs. That is why, in the bittersweet days of early November when the colours of the dying leaves are at their most intense, a visit to Lewesdon has become an annual rite of passage.

Toiling up the steep track to the summit becomes more of a challenge with each passing year, but the rewards are worth every moment of creaking knee joints: not just for the views over the Marshwood Vale, but above all for the magic of the trees themselves in all their autumn glory. Even when there is no sun to light them, they seem to give out their own pure radiance.

Already half the leaves are down. Pensioned off by their parent trees, their job is done. Now they lie in deep drifts along the aisles, piled up against mossy banks where toadstools flourish in the dampness. Mixed with the taint of rotting humus, their underworld odours cling to the nostrils: the ineluctable smell of autumn, letting us know the old year is dying.

THE tracks in the mud at the river's edge are as clear as the banner headlines in a Sunday newspaper. 'Otter,' they scream. The five webbed toes on each paw print say it all. Nothing else they could be. They are big, too. Probably left by an old dog otter checking out his territory. Otters often travel many miles during the night, swimming up one stream and then running across the fields to swim back down another tributary to rejoin the Brit.

EUROPEAN OTTER *Lutra lutra*

I try to picture him in the pool where the river bends and the brown trout hover under the willows: the smooth-as-silk body, the fierce whiskered head. That is what I remember of my first otter, seen in Strathglass in the Scottish Highlands in 1984.

I was with Sir John Lister-Kaye, one of Scotland's most eminent naturalists who had worked as a young man with Gavin Maxwell, the author whose bestselling *Ring of Bright Water* achieved for otters what Joy and George Adamson did for lions. If anyone could find me an otter it was Sir John, and I was not disappointed. In fact, on that dawn patrol up the River Glass we saw two otters, a mother and cub, and watched them romping and roistering for a full 15 minutes. Mission accomplished!

In those days, otters were unprotected by law and still legally hunted with packs of hounds; but the hunters were never their worst enemy. From the late 1950s on, they faced a far more insidious menace. Pesticides – the same toxic chemicals that were simultaneously bringing down the peregrine falcon – had begun to wipe otters off the map.

In time the worst poisons were banned and so were the hunters, and the otter has staged a remarkable nationwide comeback. Today they have reclaimed all their former haunts – including the modest little Mangerton River that flows through my orchard and down past Milton Mill, the former home of the writer and naturalist, Kenneth Allsop. Sadly, he never lived to celebrate the otter's return. But how thrilled he would have been to see those telltale tracks: positive proof that the river is in good heart again.

HOAR frost on the grass, and a robin singing in the falling leaves. To love a place truly you must know it in all its seasons. For me,

Dorset has never been just a brief summer-holiday fling, and November brings its own quiet pleasures. The days draw in, heralding a time of misty horizons and muted colours, miraculous and austere, in which the hills vanish behind grey walls of drizzle and the entire county is as sodden as an unsqueezed sponge.

Now is the time for long walks through the roadless valleys around Loscombe and Poorton, where buzzards sail over the dying bracken and there is nothing to tell you which century you are in.

The same end-of-year pleasures can be found among the stunted oaks of Powerstock Common, where the musty reek of rotting leaves clings to the nostrils. Here, the dominant tree is the oak. More than one species grows in Britain, but those on Powerstock Common are pedunculate oaks (*Quercus robur*), and possibly owe their stunted shape to having been coppiced by nibbling deer.

If allowed to live out its full span, an English oak will grow for centuries, attaining a height of as much as 130 feet (40 metres) and a girth of up to 40 feet (12 metres). No wonder these magnificent living monuments – typified by the majestic field oaks of the Marshwood Vale – are venerated in Britain as symbols of strength and endurance.

Furthermore, oaks support more life than any other of our native trees, including hundreds of insect species. Every autumn they produce vast quantities of acorns, yet few seedlings ever appear. Instead, most of them end up as a vital food source for wood pigeons, jays, squirrels, mice, deer and badgers.

WINTER is coming. I can feel it in my bones, and wildlife must make ready as best it can. For many, hibernation is nature's strategy for survival in a cold climate. As soon as the first frosts begin to bite, grass snakes and slow-worms head for the warmth of our garden compost heaps. Butterflies such as the peacock and small tortoiseshell take shelter in sheds and outbuildings, while brimstones disappear among dense ivy leaves until the returning spring.

When hedgehogs hibernate, curled up in a nest of grass and leaves from November through January, their heart rate plummets to 20 beats per minute to safely see them through the time when food is hard to come by.

All British bats also hibernate, choosing caves or cellars in which to roost instead of flying out to feed. As for the dormouse, our only true hibernating rodent, it curls up in its tight-woven nest and switches off, sleeping right through the winter until April or May.

Contrary to popular opinion, squirrels do not hibernate, although they bury caches of nuts as insurance against the hardest weather, and neither do badgers, which nevertheless spend more time underground, sleeping longer and more deeply when earthworms – their staple diet – are hard to dig from frozen ground.

DECEMBER

HOW I love the winter, when the hoar frost lingers under my garden hedge and the foxes scream in the dead of night as if crucified by cold. In many ways this is the best time of all, a connoisseur's season of muted colours in which Dorset becomes a watercolour wash of ghostly woods and bare horizons. The days may be short, but I revel in late afternoon walks among the crooked oaks of Powerstock Common before the teatime ritual of drawing the curtains to create a cave of warmth around the inglenook.

But before you put a match to the fire it is helpful to know which logs burn best. I always refer to a marvellous little booklet published in 1982 by the Harnser Press, based in Norfolk. Called *The Good Wood Guide*, it is full of helpful hints for would-be pyromaniacs.

To burn efficiently, it says, your logs should not have a moisture content of more than 20 per cent, which means they should be stored under cover for the best part of the year before they are ready.

In addition, there are general rules to follow. Hardwoods always burn the slowest. Larch, spruce, Douglas fir and Scots pine all burn fiercely but also tend to throw out sparks. Heartwood burns better than sapwood and seasoned logs are better than green.

Most interesting to my mind is its listing of our native trees and the special qualities of their timber. For instance, ash logs burn well, either wet or dry, on open fires. Beech and birch are excellent when fully seasoned. Holly and hornbeam are slow burning and long lasting. Apple and pear burn well and fragrantly, and seasonal lengths of solid oak are ideal for slow combustion.

Whichever logs you favour, the homely reek of woodsmoke carries with it the ache of nostalgia, kindling an atavistic pleasure that goes back far beyond the inglenooks of Dickensian coaching inns. And at Christmas, traditionally a time for the burning of yule logs, a wood fire seems to give out more than just a physical glow as we bask in the released energy of sunlight stored up in summers past, when we and the woods were young.

LITTLE owls are rarer these days. There was a time when they bred in the abandoned limekiln on the way to Loders, and I would often pass one perched on a fence post in broad daylight, a feathered goblin with yellow cat's eyes, or hear their shrill yelping cries at dusk.

Sadly, their numbers have declined significantly since then, not only in Dorset but all over the country. The rot set in during the 1950s and 1960s – the bad old decades of unregulated pesticides – since when intensive farming and the demolition of derelict farm buildings have further reduced their population to around 6,000 pairs. If you want to see them in Dorset today, one of the best locations is on the Isle of Portland, where they breed in the abandoned quarry workings.

Once thought sacred to the goddess Athene (their Latin name is *Athene noctua*), little owls are not native to this country. They were introduced from the continent in the late 19th century and quickly established themselves across lowland Britain.

Although most active during the night, little owls are commonly seen by day, sitting bolt upright on stone walls or gateposts, or flitting low across the fields in search of their prey: worms, beetles, small mammals, frogs, lizards and small birds. In the nesting season, which peaks around early May, four or five eggs are laid, and the young are ready to leave the nest four weeks after hatching.

A curious plant is mistletoe: a semi-parasitic evergreen that roots itself in the branches of apple, oak and poplar trees. Revered by our Celtic and Anglo-Saxon ancestors, it has since become synonymous with Christmas, when sprigs are hung up in houses all over the country. Birds love its pearly white berries, especially mistle thrushes (hence the name), that spread the plant by cleaning their beaks against a bough and leaving the sticky seeds behind.

But no other plant is more deeply entwined with the spirit of Christmas than the holly. In pagan times it was gathered to celebrate

HOLLY *Ilex aquifolium*

141

the winter solstice and when Christianity arrived, instead of dying out, the old ways were subsumed into the new religion. The holly leaves became Christ's crown of thorns; the berries were His drops of blood.

Every year as December draws on, we still gather sprigs to decorate our kitchen and hang around the inglenook at the turning of the year. And then, once Christmas has passed and each day becomes imperceptibly longer, there is the sure knowledge that already, at least down here in England's soft underbelly, spring is stirring. It will not be long before the first snowdrops appear and the whole triumphant cavalcade of the natural world will start all over again.

AFTERWORD

WHEN Coronavirus arrived in Britain, a profound change overtook the countryside. It was impossible not to be aware of it – the return of an ancient silence, the like of which I had not experienced since I first came to Dorset half a century ago.

The all-enveloping hush imposed by the nationwide policy of self-isolation magnified all the sounds of the natural world quietly going about its business, untouched by the catastrophe that had turned our own world upside down. Was it my imagination or was the dawn chorus louder than ever throughout those months? Blackbirds, thrushes, deep-throated wood pigeons all joined in – singing a song of hope and reassurance that nature was carrying on regardless of what changes were affecting the built environment of humankind.

The air was much cleaner, too; a joy to breathe. And I swear I could smell the tang of the Atlantic and its forbidden beaches, even though they are a hundred miles away.

By day, the sky was a complete vault of blue unsullied by the contrails of the grounded jetliners, and at night the stars were the brightest I had seen since I was in the Kalahari 20 years ago. The bushmen of Botswana, who believe the stars to be hunters in the heavens, say they can hear them in the profound stillness of the desert. But all I was able to pick up were the quavering voices of tawny owls in the woods behind Milton Mill.

For the time being, at least, any hopes of returning to Africa are remote in the extreme. But the silver lining to the pandemic has been the simple pleasures of a lockdown life at home: planting potatoes, seeing the first orange tip butterfly of the year and revelling, as always, in watching the first swallows, swooping over the meadows as if to confirm that for us, too, the world will eventually return to normal.

THE DORSET AONB

The Dorset Area of Outstanding Natural Beauty was designated in 1959 and is England's second biggest AONB. It covers more than 40 per cent of the county, including the lion's share of the Jurassic Coast – England's first natural World Heritage Site – which extends from Exmouth in Devon all the way to the chalk stacks of Old Harry Rocks near Poole Harbour. In short, a worthy contender to become England's next national park.

GETTING THERE

South Western Railway services run from London Waterloo to all stations between Bournemouth and Weymouth. Tel: 0345 600 0650; www.southwesternrailway.com.

Wessex Trains run regularly from Bristol Temple Meads through to Weymouth via Westbury. For more information visit www.wessextrains.co.uk or call National Rail Enquiries: tel: 0345 748 4950.

GETTING AROUND

Access the Jurassic Coast in comfort by double-decker bus with CoastlinX53. Or view Dorset's World Heritage coast from the sea. All kinds of trips from RIB rides and evening cruises to glass-bottomed boats are available on the Fleet Lagoon. Details from Traveline public transport information. Tel: 0871 200 2233; www.traveline.info and www.jurassiccoast.org.

PRICELESS WILDLIFE SANCTUARIES

The Dorset Wildlife Trust manages 42 nature reserves, and two of them – Kingcombe Meadows on the River Hooke and neighbouring Powerstock Common – were combined in June 2021 to create England's newest National Nature Reserve.

Back in 1972, not long after I first moved to live in Powerstock, I wrote about what was happening to Powerstock Common, whose 262 acres (1 square kilometre) of rough open country and ancient woodland had been leased to the Forestry Commission during the previous decade. Under the headline, 'Requiem for a forest' in the *Sunday Times* I described how the Commission appeared hell-bent on clear-felling its magical oak woods and replacing them with soulless ranks of conifers.

'A senseless environmental blitzkrieg,' I called it, and the Commissioners of the day didn't like such public criticism. They wrote to Harold Evans, the paper's editor, demanding that I should be sacked. But Harry stood firm. 'I like it when my reporters upset the establishment,' he said. And miraculously, in the years that followed, the Forestry Commission relented. What was left of the Common was spared and subsequently passed into the hands of the Dorset Wildlife Trust, who slowly brought it back to life.

In 1987 they also acquired Kingcombe ('The Farm that Time Forgot'), and today, together with the Common and its goblin oaks, its 450 acres (2 square kilometres) of ancient hedges and flower-rich hay meadows are preserved for all time – a worthy tribute to the Trust and its members who have worked so hard to sustain and enhance these priceless wildlife sanctuaries.

The reserve's showcase species include small pearl-bordered fritillaries, which can be seen on the wing in late May and June. Here, too, you will find the Kingcombe Visitor Centre (tel: 01300 320684), which offers a wide range of wildlife courses and day walks around the reserve. For further information on the Dorset Wildlife Trust and its reserves visit www.dorsetwildlifetrust.org.uk or call 01305 264620.

FURTHER READING

In the Country by Kenneth Allsop, published in 2011 by Little Toller Books, an imprint of the Dovecote Press, priced at £12.

West With The Light by Brian Jackman, published in 2021 by Bradt Guides, priced £9.99.

Wild About Britain by Brian Jackman, published in 2017 by Bradt Guides, priced £9.99.

ACKNOWLEDGEMENTS

My grateful thanks are due to all those who helped to transform ten years of what used to be called 'nature notes' into a book that more than anything represents a love letter to a very special corner of south-west England.

Foremost among them must be Anna Moores at Bradt Guides Ltd, my publisher, and Hilary Bradt, who founded the company in 1974 and who has been my most staunch supporter in this venture. Nor could this book have come into being without the eagle eye of Ross Dickinson, who edited the text and and Pepi Bluck for her layout skills.

Especial thanks must also go to Liz Somerville, the Dorset artist nonpareil, for creating the book's outstanding cover, and to Carry Akroyd for her wonderfully evocative illustrations of West Dorset's wildlife in all its glory that introduce each chapter.

Owing to the economic constraints imposed by two years of restrictions during the Covid pandemic, publication of this book could not have happened without financial assistance from a crowdfunding campaign. Those involved included Margaret Morgan-Grenville, Colin Varndell for his superb wildlife photographs, Lawrence Moore for generously allowing us to use images from *The Vale*, his DVD tribute to the Marshwood Vale and its people, and, above all, Tristan Allsop for producing the video featured in our crowdfunding campaign.

And finally, as always, my eternal thanks to Annabelle, my inspirational wife and travelling companion, who shares my passion for West Dorset's wildlife and landscapes, and never questions my long hours in front of the computer screen.

IN-CHAPTER ILLUSTRATIONS:

All from shutterstock.com:

The award-winning Slow Travel series from Bradt Guides

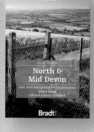
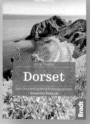

THE BRADT STORY

In the beginning

It all began in 1974 on an Amazon river barge. During an 18-month trip through South America, two adventurous young backpackers – Hilary Bradt and her then husband, George – decided to write about the hiking trails they had discovered through the Andes. *Backpacking Along Ancient Ways in Peru and Bolivia* included the very first descriptions of the Inca Trail. It was the start of a colourful journey to becoming one of the best-loved travel publishers in the world; you can read the full story on our website (www. bradtguides.com/ourstory).

Getting there first

Hilary quickly gained a reputation for being a true travel pioneer, and in the 1980s she started to focus on guides to places overlooked by other publishers. The Bradt Guides list became a roll call of guidebook 'firsts'. We published the first guide to Madagascar, followed by Mauritius, Czechoslovakia, and Vietnam. The 1990s saw the beginning of our extensive coverage of Africa: Tanzania, Uganda, South Africa, and Eritrea. Later, post-conflict guides became a feature: Rwanda, Mozambique, Angola, Sierra Leone, Bosnia and Kosovo.

Comprehensive – and with a conscience

Today, we are the world's largest independently owned travel publisher, with more than 200 titles, from full-country and wildlife guides to Slow Travel guides like this one. However, our ethos remains unchanged. Hilary is still keenly involved, and we still get there first: two-thirds of Bradt guides have no direct competition.

But we don't just get there first. Our guides are also known for being more comprehensive than any other series. We avoid templates and tick-lists. Each guide is a one-of-a-kind expression of an expert author's interests, knowledge and enthusiasm for telling it how it really is.

And a commitment to wildlife, conservation and respect for local communities has always been at the heart of our books. Bradt Guides was championing sustainable travel before any other guidebook publisher.

Thank you!

We can only do what we do because of the support of readers like you – people who value less-obvious experiences, less-visited places and a more thoughtful approach to travel. Those who, like us, take travel seriously.

Bradt GUIDES
TRAVEL TAKEN SERIOUSLY